Setting for the New York production of "Today, I Am A Fountain Pen." Designed by James Fenhagen.

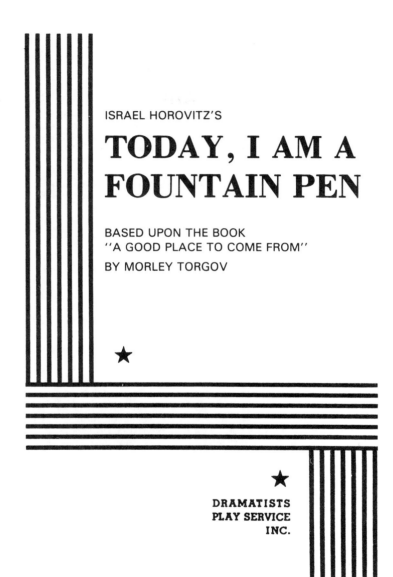

Copyright, Revised ©, 1996, by Israel Horovitz
Copyright ©, 1987, by Israel Horovitz
Based upon the book "A Good Place to Come From"
Copyright ©, 1973, by Morley Torgov

All Rights Reserved

CAUTION: Professionals and amateurs are hereby warned that TODAY, I AM A FOUNTAIN PEN is subject to a royalty. It is fully protected under the copyright laws of the United States of America, and of all countries covered by the International Copyright Union (including the Dominion of Canada and the rest of the British Commonwealth), and of all countries covered by the Pan-American Copyright Convention and the Universal Copyright Convention, and of all countries with which the United States has reciprocal copyright relations. All rights, including professional/amateur stage rights, motion picture, recitation, lecturing, public reading, radio broadcasting, television, video or sound taping, all other forms of mechanical or electronic reproduction, such as information storage and retrieval systems and photocopying, and the rights of translation into foreign languages, are strictly reserved. Particular emphasis is laid upon the question of readings, permission for which must be secured from the Author's agent in writing.

The stage performance rights in TODAY, I AM A FOUNTAIN PEN (other than first class rights) are controlled exclusively by the DRAMATISTS PLAY SERVICE, INC., 440 Park Avenue South, New York, N.Y. 10016. No professional or non-professional performance of the play (excluding first class professional performance) may be given without obtaining in advance the written permission of the DRAMATISTS PLAY SERVICE, INC., and paying the requisite fee.

Inquiries concerning all other rights should be addressed to the Author care of Dramatists Play Service, Inc.

SPECIAL NOTE

Anyone receiving permission to produce TODAY, I AM A FOUNTAIN PEN is required to give credit to the Author as sole and exclusive Author of the Play on the title page of all programs distributed in connection with performances of the Play and in all instances in which the title of the Play appears for purposes of advertising, publicizing or otherwise exploiting the Play and/or a production thereof; the name of the Author must appear on a separate line, in which no other name appears, immediately beneath the title and in size of type equal to 50% of the largest, most prominent letter used for the title of the Play. No person, firm or entity may receive credit larger or more prominent than that accorded the Author.

SPECIAL NOTE ON RADIO BROADCASTS
AND MOTION PICTURE SOUNDTRACKS

For performance of the radio broadcasts and motion picture soundtracks mentioned in this Play that are protected by copyright, the permission of the copyright owners must be obtained; or other broadcasts and motion picture soundtracks in the public domain substituted.

TAPE OF MUSICAL SELECTIONS AND SOUND EFFECTS

To obtain a tape of all musical selections and sound effects used in the original New York production of this play, please write to Aural Fixation, c/o Guy Sherman, 267 East Tenth Street, New York, N.Y. 10009.

The world premiere of TODAY, I AM A FOUNTAIN PEN was presented by the American Jewish Theatre (Stanley Brechner, Artistic Director) in New York City, January 2, 1986. It was directed by Stephen Zuckerman; the set design was by James Fenhagen; the costume design was by Mimi Maxmen; the lighting design was by Curt Ostermann; the sound design was by Aural Fixation; the casting was by Darlene Kaplan; the production photographer was Gerry Goodstein; the production stage manager was Michael S. Mantel; the production coordinator was Neal Fox. The cast was as follows:

IRVING YANOVER	Josh Blake
EMIL ILCHAK	Stephen Prutting
ARDENSHENSKY/UKRAINIAN PRIEST	Sol Frieder
MRS. ILCHAK	Dana Keeler
ESTHER YANOVER	Marcia Jean Kurtz
ANNIE ILCHAK	Melissa Leo
MOSES YANOVER	Sam Schacht
PETE LISANTI	Grant Shaud

TODAY, I AM A FOUNTAIN PEN was originally commissioned by The Community Theatre Project of the National Foundation for Jewish Culture.

TODAY, I AM A FOUNTAIN PEN was produced on the off-Broadway stage by Lou Kramer, Kenneth Waissman & Robert A. Buckley in association with Louis Scheeder, Road Works Productions, Michael Lonergan. The original cast transferred with the play, with the following exceptions: Barbara Garrick played ANNIE, Stan Lachow played ILCHAK, and Danny Gerard played IRVING.

THE PEOPLE OF THE PLAY

ESTHER YANOVER: 30's; small, somewhat round; Irving's mother.
MOSES YANOVER: 30's; a kindly face; Irving's father.
IRVING YANOVER: 10 years old; small, thin.
ANNIE ILCHAK: 15 years old; classic Ukrainian looks.
PETE LISANTI: 18 years old; athletic, Italian looks.
EMIL ILCHAK: 40; muscular, Ukrainian looks.
MRS. ILCHAK: 30's; strong-backed, Ukranian looks.
ARDENSHENSKY: an old Jew.
UKRAINIAN PRIEST: an old Ukrainian (also plays Ardenshensky).

THE TIME OF THE PLAY

1941, during the early stages of the War in Europe.

THE PLACE OF THE PLAY

The action of the play takes place in and around the home and store of the Yanover family, in Sault Ste. Marie, Ontario, Canada.

For Hannah and Oliver Horovitz, who were born during the 1st Preview of "Today, I Am A Fountain Pen." Thank you for giving your Daddy a "1st Preview Story" that no other playwright will ever top.

TODAY, I AM A FOUNTAIN PEN

The lights in the auditorium fade out.
In the darkness, we hear the sound of a child playing a Chopin etude on a piano.
A spotlight fades up on Jacob Ardenshensky, an old Jew, who speaks directly to the audience.

ARDENSHENSKY. I heard that! (*He points to man in audience.*) Not a word out of my mouth yet and that one turns to his wife and says "I hate it already" . . . (*Calls out to rear of auditorium.*) What's the matter? You've never seen a Canadian before? (*Smiles at man in audience.*) Tonight's play is called "Today, I Am A Fountain Pen" . . . (*Points at someone in audience who has laughed.*) You know the joke? (*Smiles.*) My name is Jacob Ardenshensky and I'm the oldest living man in the Soo . . . I beg your pardon. I said the Soo. (*To another man.*) . . . not "the Zoo"! The "Soo" is our nickname for Sault Ste. Marie, Ontario. That's in Canada. You've heard of Canada . . . (*To another woman.*) Don't worry, madame, we speak English . . . (*Shrugs to man in rear.*) I'm sorry, but we speak English . . . (*To all.*) My landsman up there said "Oyy, English." (*To Old Yiddle.*) It's a very easy English . . . Sault Ste. Marie, Ontario, is just across the Lake from Sault Ste. Marie, Michigan. It is now early 1941. There is a war in Europe, and the news from the front is just beginning to drift home to Canada. On the other side of the Lake, American hepcats are still cuttin' the rug to "The Flat Foot Floogee with the Floy Floy" . . . Americans. (*Lights up to glow on stage. Esther Yanover in second spotlight. Irving continues to play piano. Moses Yanover is in the store, below.*) The boy at the piano is Irving Yanover. He's ten. The boy's father, Moses Yanover, is working downstairs, in the family's drygoods store. I bought a defective sheet from Yanover many years ago, but, that's another story. Irving's mother, Esther Yanover, has something to say to you about happiness . . . (*To Esther.*) Are we ready? (*Esther nods. Ardenshensky speaks to audience.*) I think we're ready. (*Smiles.*) I'll be back later. (*Ardenshensky exits. Esther looks at audience; speaks. Music in: Chopin, played lightly on a piano by a child. Auditorium lights fade out. In a pinspot, we see the anguished face of Esther Yanover.*)

ESTHER. You want to know what happiness is. I'll tell you what happiness is: happiness is *help* . . . neither of which am I getting . . . (*Pauses.*) Buttttt. You'll never hear *meee* complain! (*Lights up full. The setting: the front rooms of the Yanover family apartment above the Yanover family store. Sault Ste. Marie, Ontario, 1941. Living room with over-stuffed furniture, old-fashioned upright piano, oversized dining table; kitchen visible* U.C. *Child's bedroom also visible. Downstairs, to one side, the store. A funnel-mouthpiece at each end of a tube creates a homemade intercom between home and store. Two smallish bells, spring-mounted, joined by lightweight chainlink, create the intercom signal. At the play's opening, Moses Yanover, fortyish, pulls the chain, causing the bell to ring in the kitchen above. Esther Yanover stands at the dining table, stuffing a chicken, enthusiastically. Yells across to mouthpiece.*) I can only put my two hands in one place at one time. (*The bell rings again.*) Stop ringing, Mosie! Stop ringing!

MOSES. Whhaaaat?

ESTHER. I said "stop ringing!"

MOSES. I stopped!

ESTHER. I'm busy stuffing tonight's chicken. Do you want help in the store, now, or supper, tonight? Make a choice!

MOSES. Help, now, and supper, later!

ESTHER. (*Suddenly yells at Irving, who sits at piano, reading a comic book.*) Irving, for God's sakes, *play!* (*Irving snaps into action. Without thought, Irving launches into Chopin "Black Keys Etude." This is clearly not the first time.*)

MOSES. Are you coming? We've got customers!

ESTHER. Three minutes! (*Esther works faster. She is aware of Irving's piano playing. She pauses to enjoy his talent.*) You play like an angel.

IRVING. Angels play harps. This is a piano . . .

ESTHER. You can't take a compliment, Mr. Wiseguy?
IRVING. I'm sorry.
ESTHER. But, Stanley Rosen: he plays like God himself.
IRVING. That's a compliment for me to take?
ESTHER. That's a *fact* for you to take!
IRVING. Stanley Rosen's four months older than me and he's a mile taller and he's been studying longer . . .
ESTHER. So, make excuses and Stanley Rosen will be playing a Steinway Grand at Carnegie Hall, New York City, and who will be his tuner?
IRVING. Great! That would make me happy. I love a good tune . . .
ESTHER. If your father or I had your Mister Wiseguy/Mister Give Up Easy Attitude, where would the store be? Where would the money for Friday night stuffed chickens be? And where, Mr. Einstein Yanover, would the money come from to pay for your *pianos*? (*Listens.*) What is that you're playing, please?
IRVING. Well, I only know scales and Chopin. I'm not playing scales, so . . . ?
ESTHER. Such a mouth on you . . . (*Sniffs, alarmed.*) What's burning? (*She runs into kitchen; disappears momentarily.*)
IRVING. Smells like bacon.
ESTHER. (*Re-appears; worried by Irving's remark.*) Are you crazy? Bacon in this house?
IRVING. I didn't say it *was* bacon. I said it *smelled* like bacon.
ESTHER. How would you know what bacon smells like?
IRVING. It's the little red bits in the Chinese food we eat at the Ritz Cafe . . .
ESTHER. Who told you that?
IRVING. God, himself: Stanley Rosen . . .
ESTHER. Mr. Rosen is having bad dreams. Whatever it is you smell, I can assure you, does not smell like bacon to you, because you have never once smelled bacon . . .
IRVING. I ate bacon at Freddy Folger's. You know that.
ESTHER. A blocked memory, believe you me . . . Eating bacon is againt the law, Mr. Jesse James, and this house does not break the law . . .
IRVING. Oh yeah, well, if the law ever changes, I would love to eat some more bacon . . . for the first time!

ESTHER. (*Turns suddenly and grabs a smoldering pot-holder; throws same into sink.*) Pot-holder! (*Lights fade up in store again.*)
MOSES. (*At intercom.*) Essie, for God's sake! I'm full of customers here!
ESTHER. I can't be everywhere, Mosie, dammit! If we had a new girl, she could be here and I could be there!
MOSES. What are you doing?
ESTHER. I'm fixing dinner and putting out fires, what do you think I'm doing?
MOSES. (*From the "store" below.*) What fires?
ESTHER. And keeping an eye on a boy who's throwing his talent *down the drain!*
IRVING. *Okay!* (*Throws his magazine down and starts playing again at once.*)
ESTHER. Potatoes! (*She grabs a burning pot from the stove; places under water.*) I cannot do it all alone! . . .
MOSES. (*From the "store" below.*) *What fires, Essie?* What are you *doing?*
ESTHER. There was a fire and it's out, Moses. Trust me! (*To Irving.*) Louder! (*To Moses.*) Happiness is help, Mosie, and I want both!
MOSES. (*From the "store" below.*) Me, too! (*Moses runs to back of store, he exits, in disgust. As he moves U., lights fade out in store, below.*)
ESTHER. That man is a genius!
IRVING. Daddy?
ESTHER. No, Chopin! (*The lights black out. Lights shift to Pete Lisanti and Annie Ilchak, teenaged. They are walking to Annie's house, holding hands, along apron of stage.*)
PETE. What if he sees us?
ANNIE. It's Wednesday. He won't be home 'til seven-thirty . . .
PETE. I guess you probably want another kiss . . .
ANNIE. Yeah, I do . . .
PETE. God! Never enough . . . (*They kiss. They are almost instantly observed from "inside the house" by Annie's father, Emil Ilchak, forty-five, powerfully built.*)
ILCHAK. (*Ukranian accent is very heavy.*) What the hell is going on here? (*Annie and Pete leap away from one another. Annie swallows a scream.*)

PETE. It's not Wednesday! It's Thursday! (*Pete runs off. Ilchak "opens the door"; speak to Annie, harshly, deep-throated anger.*)
ILCHAK. (*Thick accent.*) Get in there, you! (*The lights shift to Ilchak, Annie and Elsa, Ilchak's wife. Yanover living room is now Ilchak living room. A screen/curtain covers piano. We hear: a Caruso recording playing on old-fashioned phonograph. Annie and Elsa prepare dinner.*)
ANNIE. Can't you speak to him for me? Please?
ELSA. We have made up . . . our mind.
ANNIE. Pete was just walking me home, mama, that's all . . .
ELSA. That's all?
ANNIE. That's all . . .
ELSA. You can lie to your papa . . . you can lie to yourself . . . but, you can't lie to me, Anja. What I see, I see . . . (*Ilchak turns, faces women. He motions to Annie.*)
ILCHAK. Sit. I want you to listen . . . (*Annie sits; listens.*)
ANNIE. It's beautiful, papa . . .
ILCHAK. I'm trying to stop my anger with something beautiful. I am thinking about what you did to me . . .
ANNIE. Papa, please. I didn't do anything to you. Pete was just walking me home.
ILCHAK. Don't you open your mouth to me, you! (*To Elsa, in Ukranian, angrily.*) Tell her!
ELSA. Just listen to your papa, please . . . just listen . . .
ANNIE. I'm sorry, papa . . .
ILCHAK. In this family, we've got rules. I told you you could never again go on any date with Pete Lisanti . . . and what do you do?
ANNIE. It wasn't a date, papa . . .
ILCHAK. (*Screams.*) *What do you dooo?*
ANNIE. I'm sorry, papa . . .
ILCHAK. Of course, you're sorry. You're sorry you got *caught!*
ANNIE. No, papa, please, listen . . .
ELSA. Anja!
ILCHAK. (*Screams.*) Pete Lisanti is NOTHING to you!
ANNIE. Yes, papa . . .
ILCHAK. I have decided. School ends for you in June, anyhow, so you will stop going to school as of yesterday and start working in a nice home, as soon as we can place you . . .
ANNIE. (*Sobs.*) Noooo . . . (*Sobbing.*) Mama, please, mama . . .

ILCHAK. You cry today, but, in ten years, you'll say "I had real parents . . ." (*Elsa stares at her husband wordlessly. Annie sobs.*) I'll let it be known that you're looking for work in a good family's house . . . (*The scene shifts back to Yanover rooms. Lights up at once on Irving, standing beside piano. Moses is in chair, reading the newspaper. Esther is sewing. Esther notices Irving first. Irving prays, soft voice; a murmur. He rocks back and forth, enthusiastically.*)
ESTHER. What are you *doing*?
IRVING. Praying.
ESTHER. Praying?
IRVING. Praying.
MOSES. *What* is he doing?
ESTHER. He's praying.
IRVING. I'm praying.
MOSES. Praying?
IRVING. Praying.
ESTHER. Praying. (*There is a pause. Irving continues to mumble his prayer and "duven"—rock and sway, as might an old Jew in prayer.*)
MOSES. I don't mean to interfere. I mean, what goes on between you and God is private business . . .
ESTHER. He's driving me crazy!
MOSES. Irving, what are you praying for?
IRVING. For a nice person.
ESTHER. Of *course* she's a nice person.
IRVING. Is Mrs. Berkowitz's niece Rosie a nice person?
ESTHER. A very nice person and you shouldn't forget it!
IRVING. Nice enough to sleep with?
ESTHER. (*Holds back laugh.*) What are you saying?
MOSES. (*Holds back laugh.*) What is he saying?
IRVING. This person you've hired is going to sleep with me, right?
ESTHER. Not "*with*" you . . .
MOSES. Next to you . . .
IRVING. Same thing.
ESTHER. In the same room . . .
IRVING. It's the same thing! (*Pauses.*) If I hired some stranger to work for me who was going to sleep with you, wouldn't you pray . . . ?
MOSES. (*Interrupting.*) *Definitely!* I would definitely pray!
IRVING. Stanley says she's from Cabbagetown . . .

ESTHER. From *what*?
IRVING. That's what he said: she's from Cabbagetown, and she's going to smell bad . . .
ESTHER. Stanley Rosen said that? (*Esther and Moses exchange a glance.*)
IRVING. That's not all he said. But you don't want to know the rest . . .
MOSES. You're absolutely right. Annie Ilchak is a superb young lady. I've met her twice. I've also met her mother and her father and her six brothers and sisters . . .
IRVING. Six?
MOSES. Six.
ESTHER. She's an old hand around little Mr. Know-It-All-Big Mouths . . .
IRVING. (*Horrified.*) She *hits* kids?!
ESTHER. Who said "She hits kids!?"
IRVING. You did . . . (*Looks to Heaven.*) Do you hear what's coming into my bedroom? Do you hear what they're putting in there? (*A knock on the door. Esther and Moses stand. Irving talks to heaven.*) Pay attention, please.
ESTHER. Stop that!
MOSES. Irving, stop praying!
ESTHER. I'll get it.
MOSES. *I'll* get it! (*Stops.*) We'll all get it. Come. (*They all go to door, open same. And there stands Annie Ilchak, a fifteen-year-old Ukranian girl, pale, thin, shivering, cold; scared. Irving prays and rocks again, more enthusiastically than ever before.*)
ESTHER. Oh my God! Don't tell me you *walked*?
MOSES. In the snow?
ESTHER. Didn't your father drive you?
MOSES. I would have picked you up! (*A small silence.*) Well, come innnnn!
ESTHER. Come innnnnn! (*Annie steps into the room. Moses and Esther clear to one side: out of her way. Irving is able to see Annie for the first time. He is standing with his eyes clenched closed. Annie enters the room, sees Irving; stops. Irving opens his eyes, looks at Annie. They hold eye contact for a moment. Annie smiles. Irving looks to heaven again. Irving smiles. He looks to heaven, once again.*)
IRVING. (*To God.*) Thank you. (*Blackout. Music: Chopin. Lights up on Yanover family, Irving, Esther, and Annie seated at table*

having tea and cake. Esther pours the tea. Moses stands; Irving is in his chair.)
ESTHER. Irving is our resident standup comedian . . .
IRVING. I'm sitting down . . .
MOSES. Show her . . . stand up. (*Pulls Irving up; sits in chair.*)
IRVING. *That* was funny.
ESTHER. Every other Jewish family in Sault Ste. Marie is raising a doctor or a lawyer. Here at 7 Queen Street, we are growing ourselves a regular Fred Allen . . .
MOSES. A ten-year-old Jack Benny . . .
ESTHER. He's only ten . . .
MOSES. Ten, going on forty . . .
ESTHER. He's an only child. That's what happens . . .
ANNIE. (*To Irving.*) Are you really going into show business?
ESTHER. Over my dead body. I have a cousin on my father's side who sang in nightclubs, thank you . . .
MOSES. Irving plays piano. (*Irving stands and stares at Annie.*)
IRVING. (*To Annie.*) You've got Italian eyes.
ANNIE. *What?*
IRVING. Are you all Ukrainian, or, part Italian, too?
ANNIE. Oh, gosh, all Ukrainian . . . absolutely totally all Ukrainian. (*She giggles.*)
ESTHER. (*To Irving.*) What kind of a question is that, young man?
IRVING. Our last girl was part Italian and part Swiss. My mother used to call her "Miss Cheese with Holes." She taught me some really nifty Italian words, though. Do you know how to say "Kiss my behind" in Italian?
ANNIE. Uh, no.
MOSES. Ten years old with a mouth like a truck driver. (*Smiles.*) This he gets from my wife's family.
ESTHER. Two comedians in one house.
IRVING. Before "Miss Cheese with Holes" we had an all-Croatian girl, "Miss Spinach Pie." She taught me some really neat words, too. Maybe you could teach me some Ukrainian words?
ANNIE. Uh, well, sure, maybe, sure . . .
IRVING. Oh, swell! We once had an all-Ukrainian girl here, but she quit after a week. I only learned one thing from her . . . (*Here Irving speaks an obscenity, in Ukrainian language.*) "Sirroco

e-pee-da do-chorda." (*Annie blushes and looks away. There is an astonished glance between Esther and Moses.*)
ESTHER. Did you just say something filthy to this girl?
IRVING. (*This never occurred to him before.*) Me? I . . . filthy?
MOSES. Did you, Irving?
ESTHER. (*To Annie.*) What did he just say to you?
ANNIE. Nothing, really. Just an old-fashioned expression.
ESTHER. Is it filthy, Irving??? Answer me, Mr. Truckdriver's Mouth! It is filthy what you just said to this girl?
IRVING. (*Panicked: He doesn't know.*) I don't know, dammit!
ANNIE. (*Lying.*) No, nooo, it wasn't filthy. It was just . . . surprising . . . to hear Irving suddenly speaking like my father.
ESTHER. You never know what's coming out of this one's mouth next. You simply never know. (*To Irving.*) You owe an extra hour's practice for that scare, Mr. Foreign Language Speaker!
IRVING. I do not! That isn't fair, I . . .
MOSES. Don't talk back to your mother, please!
IRVING. You talk back to your mother! (*To Annie.*) He does. Sometimes he screams at my grandmother: loud, too.
MOSES. Your grandmother is deaf. I *have* to scream . . .
IRVING. Oh, yeah, well, how do I know that my very own mother isn't [dahbahhhh] . . . (*This last word/sound is barely audible.*)
ESTHER. That your mother isn't *what*?
IRVING. (*Screams.*) *Deaf!*
MOSES. Irving Yanover! (*Irving runs to piano.*)
IRVING. I'll practice! I'll practice! (*Lights crossfade. The Chopin continues, but on tape, through the auditorium speakers. Lights up in the bedroom. Irving is lying atop his bed; Annie is arranging things on her dresser-top. The music fades under the scene, lightly.*) Do you hate sharing a bedroom?
ANNIE. I'm used to sharing a *bed.*
IRVING. I guess that's okay if the bed's big.
ANNIE. It was pretty big . . .
IRVING. My mother and father's bed is *great.* Maybe we could share that sometime.
ANNIE. (*Looks at Irving: smiles.*) Do you do well in school?
IRVING. If I didn't, I'd be dead. You'd have the whole bedroom to yourself. I got seven "Excellents" and one "Very Good"

. . . (*Pauses in disgust.*) Stanley Rosen got eight "Excellents."
ANNIE. You really hate him, huh?
IRVING. You'll see. When you meet him, you'll hate him, too. He's a twirp and a jerk.
ANNIE. Oh, yuh. I hate twirps and jerks. (*Irving giggles approvingly.*)
IRVING. Hey maybe I could get him here for supper with his parents and you could slip some poison onto his brisket. (*Pauses.*) I'm planning to murder Stanley Rosen.
ANNIE. I can see why. Eight excellents. What a twirp!
IRVING. (*Pleased.*) Do Ukrainians really eat weird things?
ANNIE. What kind of weird things?
IRVING. Oh, well . . . like cabbage?
ANNIE. Cabbage isn't weird.
IRVING. How about bacon?
ANNIE. You think bacon is weird?
IRVING. I think bacon is wonderful, but it is totally illegal for Jews. Pig food.
ANNIE. Pig food?
IRVING. Pig food.
ANNIE. Pigs eat bacon?
IRVING. Pigs *are* bacon.
ANNIE. Right. Well, if cabbage and bacon is weird food, then I guess Ukrainians eat weird food . . . (*Annie reties the twine around her dilapidated suitcase.*)
IRVING. How come you had twine tied around your suitcase? When you first came here I noticed your suitcase was tied together with twine . . . but, when you opened it, there wasn't much in there . . . to fall out, I mean . . .
ANNIE. (*Looks at Irving; pauses.*) Better safe than sorry, I guess . . .
IRVING. How come you brought so little? The last girl needed two whole drawers, she had so much stuff.
ANNIE. I guess she was fancy.
IRVING. Nawww. She wasn't fancy. I heard my mother talking to my father about her, after she quit. She forgot some of her underwear and my mother said it was really filthy . . . (*Pauses.*) Do you think I'm really funny?
ANNIE. When I first got here I noticed your big eyes, right away, and I thought "What big eyes this little boy has!" . . . and

then I got to hear your big mouth, and I thought "What a big mouth for a little boy!" Now, I've found out that you also have inordinately big ears—they hear *every*thing, right! So, I guess it stands to reason that you've gotta have the big head you've got . . . 'cause you are really the Big Head of all time! . . . but, you've gotta have a big head, right? 'cause it's got to lug all that other BIG STUFF AROUND!
IRVING. (*Looks up to heaven.*) WHY MEEE? (*Blackout. Lights fade up in store, below. Esther yells up to Annie, over intercom.*)
ESTHER. Annnieee! I forgot to tell you that the saucepans are milk-and-meat, too. It isn't just the silverware. Are you listening? Are you listening? (*Lights fade up in Yanover home. Annie stands talking on telephone, while at the same time, trying to talk with Esther, who stands at the intercom, below, in "store", screaming up to Annie.*)
ANNIE. (*Into telephone: quietly.*) Of course, I want to see you, too . . . but . . . When? Where? . . . (*Pauses; then, in a hushed voice.*) Pete? Please, Pete . . . *Peeeeeeete.*
ESTHER. Annnie, are you listening to me?
ANNIE. (*Yells out.*) Yes, Mrs. Yanover, I'm listening! (*Into telephone.*) I have to go, Pete . . .
ESTHER. My grandmother (Alivoh, Shalom) knew a woman in Pinsk, who dressed impeccably, but kept a wreck of a saucepan for her gravies . . .
ANNIE. Please, Pete, let me call you back . . .
ESTHER. Annnie, are you talkingggg? Annnieee? (*Esther pulls the bell-cord, below, the bell rings in kitchen.*)
ANNIE. (*Yells out.*) I'm not talking, Mrs. Yanover. I'm listening to you! (*Into telephone.*) Pete, I have to go, *please!*
ESTHER. It sounded like you said something.
ANNIE. I'm listening! (*Into telephone.*) 'Bye, Pete. I miss you . . . (*Hangs up; yells out.*) Whhhhat-ttt, Mrs. Yanoverrrr? I can't hear youuuu!
ESTHER. (*Over intercom.*) Shh. Not so loud, Annie! There are customers! Did you hear what I said about separate milk and meat saucepans?
ANNIE. (*Continues to yell into intercom.*) Oh I heard most of it.
ESTHER. (*Into intercom, as well.*) You didn't hear all of it?
ANNIE. I was dusting in the front room . . .
ESTHER. I gave an entire Kosher-lesson . . .

ANNIE. Well I heard *most* of it . . .
ESTHER. You have to know it *all*! You can't make mistakes in a Kosher home! (*Pauses; listens.*) Why isn't Irving practicing? It's after three-thirty!
ANNIE. I think he's in the bathroom.
ESTHER. Is he sick?
ANNIE. He might be reading.
ESTHER. Go look.
ANNIE. I'll call him.
ESTHER. You tell him I said that school holidays are not holidays from practicing. His closest friend, Stanley Rosen, you can assure him for me, is not in the bathroom, at this time. Stanley is at the piano and he is playing *scales*! CAN YOU HEAR ME, ANNIEEE?
ANNIE. (*Starting to frazzle.*) I HEAR YOU, MRS. YANOVER! (*Annie, in Esther Yanover's spirit, screams out to Irving.*) *IRVVVINNNNNNNNG! GET OUT OF THE BATHROOOMMMM!* (*The door pops open and Irving, frightened, looks at Annie.*)

IRVING. Jesus, Annie, what's the matter?	ESTHER. (*From downstairs.*) Not so loud, Annie! We've got customers!

(*There is a pause. The telephone rings. Annie turns, horrified, and stares at the telephone. It rings again.*)
ESTHER. Who's on the phone? (*No reply.*) *Who's on the phone?* (*Annie, in a panic, picks up the receiver and, immediately, hangs up, without answering.*)
ANNIE. (*Calls out to Mrs. Yanover.*) Wrong number! (*To Irving; an authorial scream.*) Practice your scales, now! That was NOT Pete Lisante! (*Irving, terrified, plays scales. Esther calls to Annie, from store below.*)
ESTHER. Annnieeee, please, come down here now . . . (*Lights fade out in Yanover home; fade up in store. Annie runs around the set and enters store, breathlessly, still carrying dishtowel. Esther greets her, smiling. The Kosher-lesson continues.*) It's quiet in the store. We can go on with our lesson, face to face . . . (*Hands Annie a pencil and paper.*) Maybe you should take notes . . .
ANNIE. I'll remember . . .
ESTHER. No, no, no. My mother made me take notes and I remembered. These laws have survived for thousands and

thousands of years because young women were made to take notes . . .
ANNIE. I'll take notes . . . (*Annie stands poised with pencil and paper. Esther gathers her thoughts.*)
ESTHER. Now these dietary laws were first devised by the Jews because the Pagans used to slaughter animals and offer them in sacrifice in the own animal's mother's milk . . .
ANNIE. They *what?*
ESTHER. I know. I remember when my mother first told me. I thought she was making it up . . . are you writing?
ANNIE. They put the animals in the animal's own mother's milk?
ESTHER. It's hard to believe that people can be so cruel. Believe me, Annie, life is not like the moving-pictures. Life does not invent such happy endings . . .
ANNIE. (*Lost in thought; a word escape.*) Yessss . . .
ESTHER. What "yes"?
ANNIE. Hmmm?
ESTHER. You said "yes" . . .
ANNIE. Oh, nothing, I was just concentrating hard on the Kosher lesson . . .
ESTHER. (*Delighted.*) You were?
ANNIE. I was.
ESTHER. It's nice having a girl in the house, Annie. Girls pay attention . . .
ANNIE. It's nice being in a house with so few children. When I told Irving that I have four brothers and two sisters, he said to me "there are too many children in your family."
ESTHER. He's got such a mouth on him . . .
ANNIE. Nooo, I think he's right!
ESTHER. Let me tell you what my grandmother told me. My grandmother would never count up the number of grandchildren she had. She thought it was bad luck. When anybody would ask her how many grandchildren she had, she would say "A lot of grandchildren." (*Smiles; remembers.*) When Mr. Yanover and I were getting married, I asked my grandmother what she thought would be the ideal number of children for a family to have . . . and she said "Estellah, the ideal number of children to have is the number of children you will get." I was panicked. "Grand-

mother? What does that *mean*?" And she said "It will become obvious." And she was right. (*Touches Annie's shoulder, lightly.*) My family is ideal and your family is ideal . . . and with you staying here with this family, it's even more ideal . . . (*The two women exchange a loving glance.*) Let me tell you the truth: the main reason we keep Kosher today is because our parents would *kill* us if we didn't! And this is reason enough . . .

ANNIE. Should I write that down?

ESTHER. No. There are some things that should *never* be written down.

ANNIE. And that's one of them?

ESTHER. And that's one of them . . . (*Blackout. On the radio, playing in room, softly, we hear: "The Fred Allen Show."* After it is established, we hear Moses's voice, offstage, calling to Irving.*)

MOSES. (*In dark.*) Irving Yanover, it's a quarter-to-nine on a school night! I want that radio turned off!

IRVING. (*In dark.*) It's Fred Allen, poppy!

MOSES. (*In dark.*) Did you hear me?

IRVING. (*In dark.*) Okay, okayyy! (*The radio switches off. There is a moment of silence, and then lights up in living room. Irving at piano; Annie housecleaning.*)

ANNIE. (*Yelling into intercom.*) Yes, Mrs. Yanover! I did it already, Mrs. Yanover . . . (*Annie stuffs her dish-towel into intercom; looks over at Irving, who laughs, conspiratorily.*)

IRVING. Annie?

ANNIE. What? (*He sits on table.*) Off the table!

IRVING. (*He sits on chair.*) You know who I want to be like when I grow up?

ANNIE. (*Sits.*) Who?

IRVING. More than anybody in all of Canada . . . in all the world . . . in the whole solar system!

ANNIE. Who?

IRVING. (*Simply.*) Horowitz.

ANNIE. (*Simply.*) Who's Horowitz?

IRVING. Who is Horowitz? Are you kidding me? Horowitz is just the single greatest pianist on the Planet Earth, that's all . . .

ANNIE. Oh, right. Horowitz. There's a Horowitz on the hockey team with my friend Pete . . .

*See Special Note on copyright page.

IRVING. That's Berkowitz. Fat Rosie Berkowitz's cousin, Arnold. He plays hockey, yuh . . . (*Pauses.*) There's a problem.
ANNIE. Huh?
IRVING. My growing up like Horowitz. Horowitz looks like a bird.
ANNIE. So do you . . .
IRVING. Yuh, but I've got big muscles. Horowitz is skinny as a rail. You should see him . . .
ANNIE. How's you get to meet him?
IRVING. I didn't! I saw him in a newsreel at the Algoma Cinema . . . I love movies. You?
ANNIE. Oh, I do.
IRVING. If I push my arm up, like this, my muscles aren't bad. Stanley Rosen has got arms like turds . . . Fingers like turds, too. He's disgusting. A real stinker! . . . (*Irving giggles.*)
ANNIE. Irvvingggg, shushhhhh! (*She giggles, too.*) Do your parents take you to the movies a lot?
IRVING. (*Ironically.*) Oh, yuh sure . . . (*Pauses.*) Twice, maybe, in my life. They are always working or else they go out to supper with the Rosens. Working and eating: that's about it . . . and yelling at me . . . (*Pauses.*) I went with my class. There was a movie about Chopin and a short with Horowitz playing Chopin. It was excellent.
ANNIE. Your parents aren't against you going to the movies?
IRVING. Naw, they're too busy working, eating and yelling . . . (*Pauses.*) Are you thinking what I'm thinking?
ANNIE. I think so. We could ask her.
IRVING. *Him*, ask him. If you ask her, she's liable to say "It would have been okay with me, but, your father said no" . . . and then he'll back her up. But, if you ask him first, he'll say "yes" and she'll have no choice . . . (*Explains.*) They both hate to be the one who says "no" . . . but he hates it much much more than she hates it. It's exhausting, figuring these things out . . . (*Pauses.*) Can you keep a secret?
ANNIE. What do you think?
IRVING. I think you can, but, you've got to say it yourself, or you're not bound.
ANNIE. I promise. (*He moves close to Annie.*)
IRVING. It's about my piano playing . . .
ANNIE. You really hate it?

19

IRVING. Opposite. I would rather be playing piano than anything else in life. But, you can't let my parents know this, okay?
ANNIE. I don't get it.
IRVING. Well, think about what my parents make me do when they punish me for something bad . . .
ANNIE. (*Smiles.*) Oh, you are very smart.
IRVING. If they knew, I'd be washing dishes, taking out garbage . . .
ANNIE. You mean the things I do . . .
IRVING. You get paid. I just get yelled at . . . Do you know Mr. Ardenshensky?
ANNIE. Who's he?
IRVING. The oldest living person in the Soo, next to his wife . . .
ANNIE. His wife is older? (*He puts his arm around Annie.*)
IRVING. Many years older. I just heard about it. Mr. Ardenshensky married a woman ten years older than him . . . and it worked out great. They just had their sixtieth anniversary . . .
ANNIE. Sixtieth. My goodness. Let's see. Twenty-five is silver, fifty is gold . . . what's sixty?
IRVING. I think sixty is bacon.
IRVING. (*Laughs; hugs Irving.*) You are the funniest boy in the whole world, Irving. *The* funniest. (*Footsteps are heard on stairs in kitchen.*)
IRVING. (*Suddenly.*) Oh, God! (*He whips around and starts playing Chopin. Annie grabs the dishtowel from the funnel. Esther Yanover enters the kitchen from downstairs.*)
ESTHER. Could you not hear me yelling?
ANNIE. Did you call?
ESTHER. Could you not hear me?
ANNIE. Maybe Irving's practicing too loudly—
IRVING. What? You say something? Oh, hiii, mama. I didn't hear you come in . . .
ESTHER. Mr. Lies-to-His-Own-Mother! You heard me! (*Goes to intercom.*) What is the matter with this thing? It was completely dead. I couldn't hear a peep; and I screamed into it fifty times . . . (*Ear to intercom.*) I can hear customers . . . (*She rings bell, testing it. Moses goes to intercom, downstairs in "store".*)
MOSES. What? I'm busy with customers . . .

ESTHER. Testing, one two three four . . .
MOSES. Why are you playing games? We've got customers!
ESTHER. Cancel the call, Mosie. Go back to the customers . . . (*He does; Esther turns to Irving.*) One extra hour of practice. (*Irving playacts great anger. He punches the keyboard six times; shouts.*)
IRVING. NO NO NO NOOOOOOO!
ESTHER. Yes, yes, yes yesssssssss! (*Annie turns away; giggles.*)
IRVING. This is the most unfair thing on the Planet Earth!
ESTHER. One more word from you and it goes up to one hour and fifteen minutes.
IRVING. *YOU WOULDN'T DARE!!!*
ESTHER. (*Shocked.*) I wouldn't *what???*
IRVING. You heard me!
ESTHER. And I'll continue to hear you: practicing . . . for one hour and thirty minutes, until the store closes at 5 p.m. (*The bell rings at intercom.*)
MOSES. (*From downstairs.*) Essie, for God's sake! It's packed down here . . .
ESTHER. Coming, Mosie. I'm going to tell you something about your son . . . if you dare to listen! (*She turns to Irving.*) I dare . . . and he will dare.
IRVING. An hour and a half?
ESTHER. An hour and a half. Want to try for two? (*Irving covers his mouth with one hand, to prevent himself from talking . . . so to speak. With the other hand, he plays Chopin. Esther nods triumphantly to Irving, and then to Annie. And then she exits. Irving continues to practice with one hand. He stares at Annie. Annie stares at Irving. She is dumbfounded. She holds back her laugh for a count of four . . . and then she explodes into laughter. The lights crossfade to store. Moses is stocking shelves. Annie enters with a glass of tea and a biscuit. She is prepared to outsmart Moses.*)
ANNIE. I'd like to talk with you about Irving, Mr. Yanover.
MOSES. (*Looking up.*) Oh. Certainly, Annie.
ANNIE. I like him a great deal, you know.
MOSES. And he you. I can tell.
ANNIE. I think that Irving stays inside too much. With you and Mrs. Yanover in the store all the time, he just stays upstairs, by himself . . . never in the air . . . and all.
MOSES. It's true, Annie . . .

ANNIE. I was thinking that I should include him in on some of my plans . . . maybe even think things up that he and I could do together . . . outside . . . in the air and all . . .
MOSES. Sounds good. What sort of things, for example?
ANNIE. . . . Walks. We could walk together. I have an idea! Irving and I could walk to the movies on Saturday. He said he loves the movies. And I'm sure he wouldn't mind walking down and back. And I wouldn't mind going at all . . .
MOSES. That sounds fine . . .
ANNIE. There's an excellent double bill playing at the Algoma on Saturday. We could be back in plenty of time for me to help with supper . . .
MOSES. Fine. I think that's a fine idea . . .
ANNIE. You do?
MOSES. Yes I do. I'll treat you both.
ANNIE. You will?
MOSES. Absolutely. My pleasure . . . Have you mentioned this plan to Mrs. Yanover?
ANNIE. Oh, not yet. Should I?
MOSES. Uh, no . . . I'll handle it. Sometimes there's a way of introducing a new idea to people without actually announcing it. The trick is to make them think the idea is theirs, and not yours . . . (*Smiles.*) It's a system that's worked quite well over the last ten years with Irving, especially . . . When I want him to read a particular book, I never say "Irving, read this, it's great!" That would guarantee that he'd read five pages and hate it. Instead, I usually say something like "What a great book! It's way too hard for a ten-year old. But you might want to take a peek at it in five or six years!" (*Smiles.*) He'll have the book read cover to cover by noon, the next day . . . (*Pauses; exact same "reading" as Irving's of same line.*) It's exhausting, figuring these things out . . . (*Smiles.*) I'll take care of the movie, okay?
ANNIE. Okay. (*Annie exits. The Chopin continues, lightly, the lights crossfade again to living room; Esther, reading. Moses enters from store.*)
MOSES. I had a very interesting talk with Annie, earlier . . .
ESTHER. And?
MOSES. She thinks Irving's looking a little pale.
ESTHER. Pale?
MOSES. Well he isn't rosy-cheeked . . .

ESTHER. It's Canada. It's twenty below zero ...
MOSES. He is indoors all the time ...
ESTHER. It's the middle of the winter ...
MOSES. Some kids skate or play hockey ...
ESTHER. What are you saying, Moses? Didn't Elsa Berkowitz's son fall through the ice?
MOSES. I'm not suggesting he take up hockey ...
ESTHER. I didn't think so!
MOSES. Walks ... *(Esther looks up.)* We're indoors all the time. He could go for walks.
ESTHER. With who?
MOSES. Annie volunteered ...
ESTHER. To walk with Irving?
MOSES. To the movies ...
ESTHER. An outdoor movie?
MOSES. To the Algoma, on Saturday. There's a John Wayne and a Roy Rogers on a double-bill, for young people ...
ESTHER. Well, I personally wouldn't allow it, but, if you've said "yes" already, I'll go along ... *(Moses starts to speak, thinks better of it. Esther and Moses look at one another. A brief pause. The music stops. The lights crossfade to bedroom to Irving and Annie atop their beds. Irving is ecstatic.)*
IRVING. I can't believe you got permission! Did you have to lie?
ANNIE. I don't lie.
IRVING. Never?
ANNIE. Never. *(And with that, Annie leans over and switches out the bedlamp between them. Lights out. There is a pause. Annie switches light on again. Irving is startled.)* Irving.
IRVING. What?
ANNIE. I did lie a little.
IRVING. I was worried, 'cause I lie a lot ... all the time! What did you lie a little about?
ANNIE. Pete Lisanti....
IRVING. Who's Pete Lisanti?
ANNIE. My boyfriend. He's going to the movie with us ...
IRVING. *(Not the best news he's ever heard.)* He is?
ANNIE. I left that part out with your father ...
IRVING. With me, too ...

ANNIE. Is it okay?
IRVING. I guess. If he's *your* boyfriend, he's my boyfriend, too . . .
ANNIE. My parents would kill me if they found out . . .
IRVING. Why?
ANNIE. They made me promise I wouldn't go out with him . . .
IRVING. You're going to break your promise?
ANNIE. Well, yuh . . . sometimes you get pushed into making promises you really never want to make in the first place . . .
IRVING. Sure, well, *sure*. But, a promise is a promise . . . (*Pete appears on stage,* D. *of Annie and Irving, in the shadows.* N.B. Room will soon become the cinema. *Neither Annie nor Irving acknowledge Pete's presence, as yet.*)
ANNIE. It's different. Pete's my boyfriend . . .
IRVING. I guess.
ANNIE. I mean really my *boyfriend*. (*Pete steps* U. *to Annie, touches her cheek with his hand. She doesn't turn, but, instead, reaches up and touches his hand on her cheek.*)
IRVING. You mean *dates*!
ANNIE. Dates. Dances . . . long walks . . .
IRVING. I know about those things . . .
ANNIE. Pete's a genius.
IRVING. Pete's a genius?
ANNIE. At hockey. He played for Tech until he graduated last year. His line was the best, two years straight, and he was the highest scorer, too . . .
IRVING. Did he go to the university?
ANNIE. Nooo, silly. He works nights at Algoma Steel, and he practices and plays during the daytime. He starts for the James Street Aces . . . He's the youngest starter . . .
IRVING. With Arnold Berkowitz.
ANNIE. When he makes the Detroit Red Wings, we're going to get married and move out of the Soo. (*Irving now turns and stares at Pete.*)
IRVING. Does Pete like you a lot?
ANNIE. I think so.
IRVING. I like you a lot, too, you know . . .
ANNIE. Pete likes me in the romantic way . . .
IRVING. Oh, right . . . (*Annie and Irving walk from bedroom, put on coats, move* D. *to Pete in area designated as lobby of Algoma Cinema.*

Lights shift with them. In the background, we hear the soundtrack from a segment of "Movietone News."*
ANNOUNCER'S VOICE. (*Offstage.*) "English and Canadian troops are known for their serious fighting spirit, but not so for our friends from down-under in Australia. Wherever the Aussie troops have gone, they have given rise to stories of their high spirits and high jinks . . .
ANNIE. Irving, this is Pete; Pete, this is Irving . . .
IRVING. Annie talks about you all the time . . . She's told me *every*thing . . .
PETE. Don't believe it.
IRVING. I shouldn't have. You're a lot shorter than I thought . . .
ANNIE. Irving's got a lot of crust . . .
PETE. You're a lot tougher than I thought . . .
IRVING. This'll be rich . . . (*Sees the joke coming.*) How so?
PETE. I always thought of kids who play the piano in a certain way.
IRVING. Sissies?
PETE. Well, no, I wouldn't say "sissies," exactly . . .
IRVING. Jerks?
PETE. That's it: jerks. You must be a dinger of a pianist.
ANNIE. Oh, he is, Pete, really. You've just got to hear Irving play . . .
IRVING. You would?
PETE. You'd better believe it. I'll make a deal. I get to hear you play piano and you get to watch me play hockey . . .
IRVING. Great!
ANNIE. Pete's a genius at hockey! And Irving's a genius at piano, Pete, he really is . . .
PETE. Well, this is a historic meeting, two geniuses shake . . .
(*They pump hands. Irving laughs. Lights flicker. We are now in the movie theatre. Irving slides between Annie and Pete. We hear: the sound of a John Wayne movie on tape,* and the lights flicker on the three of them, brightly, as they watch the movie, seated in a straight line, eyes straight ahead, staring widely. Pete's arm sneaks out around Annie. Irving sees; leans back against it. The film's soundtrack continues. Irving turns, discreetly, and stares at Pete's hand on Annie's shoulder, next to Irving's*

---

*See Special Note on copyright page.

young face. Irving looks up at them as Annie and Pete face one another and kiss, deeply, passionately. Irving stares at them. Annie breaks from the kiss, somehow aware of Irving's staring. Pete pulls back, surprised. They whisper to one another.)
ANNIE. Are you hungry?
PETE. You want some popcorn?
IRVING. I wouldn't mind.
PETE. My treat.
IRVING. You sure?
PETE. Sure, I'm sure . . .
VOICE. (*From the darkness.*) Shhhhhh . . .
SECOND VOICE. (*From the darkness.*) Shhhhhh . . .
IRVING. (*Takes money.*) I'll be right back . . . (*Irving stands and walks out of the "row," whispering "Excuse me" as he goes. The lights (film) continue their flicker. The soundtrack continues, softly. Annie and Pete kiss again, now certain that Irving isn't with them, staring. Their kiss is long, deep, passionate. Their hands search each others' bodies. The lights crossfade to the living room. Irving sits reading a comic book. Esther stands ironing shirts.*)
ESTHER. To me, a movie in the daytime is like eating chicken for breakfast.
IRVING. What's wrong with chicken for breakfast?
ESTHER. Don't talk disgusting.
IRVING. I think it's important for people to be prepared to eat new things . . . That's how you got me to eat squash. I hated squash, but, you convinced me to try . . .
ESTHER. I thought you still hated squash.
IRVING. That's not the point.
ESTHER. Tomorrow morning you get two scrambled eggs and one drumstick . . .
IRVING. Did you ever break a promise, Mama?
ESTHER. I would rather break an arm than a promise. Why?
IRVING. You never EVER broke a promise?
ESTHER. Not a promise that counted . . .
IRVING. What promises count and what promises don't count?
ESTHER. What are you getting at, Mr. Beat-Around-The-Bush? What have you done?
IRVING. I'm just asking.
ESTHER. About what?
IRVING. Bacon.

ESTHER. You ate bacon???
IRVING. I didn't! I didn't! I'd just like to know why I can't!
ESTHER. You have a funny way of asking . . .
IRVING. Why can't I?
ESTHER. Because my mother, your grandmother (Alivoh, Shalom) and your father's mother, your own grandmother, both made me promise that I would keep a Kosher home and to bring you up Jewish, and I promised, and that promise counts . . . So there'll always be Jews.
IRVING. There'll always be Jews, Mama, with or without bacon . . .
ESTHER. Mr. Know-It-All. You've read the papers? You know what's happening in Europe?
IRVING. You mean to tell me, mama, that if I eat bacon, there will be no more Jews in Europe?
ESTHER. Europe . . . North America, South America . . . the Planet Earth. That, my son, is exactly, what I mean to tell you . . . (*Suddenly.*) Are you watching the time? (*Irving runs into kitchen; looks at clock.*)
IRVING. Oh, God, I'm late! (*Irving stands and runs to his coat. Esther helps bundle him up against the cold. Lights crossfade again: Lights and sound full again now in "cinema." Pete and Annie break from their embrace. Annie looks around for Irving. Irving squeezes into "row" carrying box of popcorn. He sits beside Annie. She smiles at him; leans over, kisses his cheek. Pete tussles Irving's hair. The three of them — Pete, Irving, Annie — stare straight ahead, wide-eyed, into the flickering light, and final dialogue of film, watching the film play out to its conclusion. Lights shift to stage apron. Irving, Pete and Annie, walk home from Algoma Cinema. Irving walks ahead, chatting, happily. Pete and Annie hold hands, nuzzle, giggle, absorbed in one another, somewhat oblivious to Irving's chirping chat.*) That was my third movie with John Wayne . . .
PETE. My second . . .
ANNIE. *Our* second . . .
PETE. *Our* second.
IRVING. In all three movies he gets married at the end, but, to different women. You would think he could just stick with one, huh? My parents say that a man shouldn't get married unless he has one thousand dollars in his bank account. How much do you have in yours, Pete?

PETE. Well, not *quite* a thousand . . .
ANNIE. A thousand dollars?
PETE. (*Ironically.*) I may have to work some overtime at the plant . . .
ANNIE. (*Smiles.*) I could save up a thousand, easy. 'Course it'd take me about six and a half years . . .
IRVING. Yuh, I'm nowhere near (a thousand) myself. I've got forty-three dollars and thirty cents saved, but that's going to piano lessons in Montreal. I'm going to study piano in Montreal, after university . . . You need a lot of money for university, too. That's why you shouldn't have too many children. How many children do you want, Pete?
PETE. Oh, I dunno', fifty . . . sixty . . .
ANNIE. *Peeeeeetttte!*
PETE. Why? I *like* kids!
IRVING. Come on, Pete, get serious. You could never have fifty or sixty kids. You'd wreck your hands, spanking them all . . . (*Giggles.*) I'll bet Pete's gonna' spank his kids, huh?
ANNIE. Pete would never!
IRVING. Me, neither . . .
PETE. There's no need to hit a kid when all's ya' hav'ta' do, really, is turn him upside-down . . . (*Pete lifts Irving upside-down, holds him by his feet.*)
IRVING. Nice . . .
ANNIE. Pete!
IRVING. I really hate this . . .
PETE. (*Self-announcing.*) And Pete Lisanti, ladies and gentlemen, turns the kid right-side-up, quick as a Shick! (*Pete rights Irving.*)
IRVING. You'll make tremendous amounts of money, when you're a pro. I've read that many hockey players earn more than two thousand in just one season . . .
PETE. Oh, that's for sure. Eddie Shore made nearly ten thousand dollars last year alone . . .
IRVING. (*Whistles.*) Ten thousand dollars? Whewww! You could get married five time more than John Wayne! Got your scarf! (*Irving grabs Pete's scarf; runs off. Pete chases. Lights crossfade to Emil Ilchak. Ilchak talks to Annie from across stage.*)
ILCHAK. So, do you like your job, Anja? (*Annie stands, moves*

to her father, who enters carrying lunch-pail; end of workday.)
ANNIE. Yes, I do, very much . . .
ILCHAK. So, your papa knows something, yes?
ANNIE. Oh, yes, it was a good idea.
ILCHAK. And the Yanovers? It's a good family?
ANNIE. A *wonderful* family.
ILCHAK. I knew, from the beginning, that this job was going to work out. You cried and your Mama yelled, but I knew. A father knows what is best for his Annie. (*Father and daughter embrace. Lights shift to store. Moses Yanover is stocking a shelf with boxes of fresh, new merchandise. It is Sunday. Irving is offstage, at the start of the scene, about to enter from the store's inventory closet with an armload of boxes. Moses calls off, to his son.*)
MOSES. Spending my Sundays stocking shelves is one of my least favorite things about being in the dry goods business. I need you to read the number on this box for me. My eyes are gone . . . (*Irving enters, carrying boxes, which he places on counter.*)
IRVING. Which shelf?
MOSES. Top shelf, . . .
IRVING. 640.
MOSES. Are you *kidding*? 640 is women's support hose and garter-belts . . . Oy vay . . . Middle-age is no picnic. First, the eyes; then, the mind . . . (*Irving reads number on box; laughs.*) It's not funny. (*Moses takes boxes down from shelf. Irving giggles.*) Imagine when Mr. Weisman gets home with what he thinks are his "ususal" boxer shorts and Mrs. Weisman unpacks . . .
IRVING. (*Interrupting, happily.*) What? What? Ladies tights?
MOSES. Worse! (*Laughs.*)
IRVING. A garter belt?
MOSES. A dozen garter belts! (*Irving and Moses share a long laugh.*) I'm glad that you spend Sundays with me. Otherwise, the day would be wasted . . . (*Smiles.*) But, this I like: just the two of us: two fellas . . . every Sunday morning . . .
IRVING. Can I ask you a question, Poppy? Fella' to fella'?
MOSES. Sure.
IRVING. How can you tell when somebody's in love?
MOSES. Somebody?
IRVING. Somebody. How can you tell?
MOSES. Oh, sometimes, somebody's knees can get all wobbly

when somebody looks at the somebody somebody's in love *with*. 'Course, it depends on a lot of things. I mean, there's Love and there's *Love*.
IRVING. Oh, I mean *Love*. People who get married sort of thing, like you and Mama. Do your knees go all wobbly when you look at her?
MOSES. Well, I . . . sometimes, sure.
IRVING. But not all the time?
MOSES. No, I would have to say no. But, this is strictly fella'-to-fella' talk . . . I mean, I wouldn't mention to your mother that I said that my knees didn't wobble all the time when I looked at her . . . and then there's the matter of your mother's knees which certainly don't wobble every time she looks across at me, either . . .
IRVING. So, love is a now-and-then wobble?
MOSES. That's it, precisely . . .
IRVING. I thought so.
MOSES. You know it's wonderful for me, Irving . . . watching you . . . being with you. (*Smiles.*) Some day you will be quite a fountain pen.
IRVING. Yuhh . . . (*Looks up; admits.*) . . . I don't get it. (*Pauses; exclaims.*) Fountain pen?
MOSES. You mean you don't know the story? Your cousin Quentin?
IRVING. Who's cousin Quentin?
MOSES. He's really *my* cousin. Your second cousin on my mother's side of the family . . . a real *schmendrick*, Quentin. What Stanley Rosen is to you, Quentin Becker was to me.
IRVING. A bedbug.
MOSES. *Two* bedbugs. (*Irving giggles.*) My uncle Sam Becker made money, so when schmendrick Quentin was *bar mitzvahed*, it was a huge affair. Every Jew in Toronto, plus most of the Gentiles. My own bar mitzvah was thirty-five Jews at a dollar a head, so I was a little jealous . . . Anyway the standard Bar Mitzvah present in those days was a fountain pen. I don't know why. It was the custom. If forty people came to your Bar Mitzvah, you could count on getting thirty fountain pens . . . which you would exchange in the shops later for something you wanted. Quentin must have gotten two hundred and fifty fountain pens.

30

IRVING and MOSES. (*In unison; Moses stays put; Irving crosses to bedroom.*) That sounds like an exaggeration, but he certainly had his pockets crammed full of fountain pens when he stood up to make his speech . . . (*Lights crossfade, to bedroom. Irving takes over the telling of the story, nearing its completion. He enters bedroom, where Annie is in her bed ready for sleep. When Irving reaches his bed, he will snap on the bedlamp, so as to be certain that the best part of the story is heard properly by his audience: Annie.*)

IRVING. You wouldn't know this on your own, but, it's the tradition that every Bar Mitzvah boy makes a speech to the congregation which has to start with the words: "Today I am a Man," because on the day of a boy's Bar Mitzvah, he, legally, in the Jewish laws, becomes a man. He becomes a full member of the congregation. He gets to sit downstairs with the men, because he's one of them. (*Suddenly.*) Are you *awake*? (*Irving leans over to Annie, who has been drifting into sleep.*) Annie!

ANNIE. I'm listening! [I'm listening!]

IRVING. I'm just getting to the best part.

ANNIE. I'm listening.

IRVING. *So.* There's Quentin . . . pockets stuffed with pens . . . standing up in front of five hundred people . . . sweating like a disgusting pig and he screams out with this dopey voice of his "Todayyyy . . . I ammm . . . a *fountain pennn*!"

ANNIE. He didn't?

IRVING. He did! (*Annie and Irving roar with laughter.*)

ANNIE. It sounds like you and your father had a wonderful time together . . .

IRVING. Oh, yuh, we always do . . . It's more than wonderful. It's actually *two*derful.

ANNIE. (*Laughs.*) I think you're *ten*derful.

IRVING. Oh, yuh, well then you're twentderful . . . (*They both laugh again.*) What's Pete?

ANNIE. Oh, Pete's a *hundra*ful . . .

IRVING. (*Slightly depressed by this computation.*) Yuh, I guess . . . (*Pauses.*) How come your father doesn't like Pete?

ANNIE. 'Cause, Pete's Italian. My father thinks the Italians keep the Ukrainians poor. The Italians control all the work at Algoma Steel and force Ukrainians into terrible jobs . . .

IRVING. Is that true?

ANNIE. I don't think it's true . . . (*Pauses.*) God, don't ever let

on I said that! Can you keep a secret?
IRVING. Do I look like I can't?
ANNIE. I know you can. (*Whispers.*) I think my father's totally wrong. I think the Italians are fine people. I've met Pete's mother and father and his brother Robert, and his sister Carmella, and they're really all fine people.
IRVING. So, why don't you bring your father to meet them?
ANNIE. Oh, don't talk crazy! My father won't have anything to do with anything that's Italian, period.
IRVING. I thought you said he loves opera?
ANNIE. He loves opera more than he loves me or my mother or anything else in the whole world . . . on the Planet Earth!
IRVING. But, all the great operas are Italian!
ANNIE. No, they're not, silly! They're Canadian . . .
IRVING. They are not. They're Italian.
ANNIE. Irving, don't say that. My father would never listen to an opera if it were Italian . . .
IRVING. Annie, I should know, right. Music is my middle name . . .
ANNIE. Irving, are you trying to kid me? Because, if you are, this isn't very funny!
IRVING. I swear to you: Verdi, Puccini . . . all of them: Italians . . .
ANNIE. The names *sound* Italian . . .
IRVING. Because they're Italian. I swear to you. I promise never to eat bacon when I grow up, if I'm lying. (*Pauses; whispers.*) I'm planning to eat a great deal of bacon when I'm a man on my own . . . which is something *my* parents made *me* promise not to do . . . like your not seeing Pete, ever . . .
ANNIE. Oh, God, this is incredible news . . .
IRVING. I'm glad I was able to tell you . . .
ANNIE. Me, too. I really owe you a lot, Irving . . . (*Pauses.*) Irving?
IRVING. What?
ANNIE. You must never, ever in a million years let on that it was me who let on, but, your parents eat bacon all the time . . .
IRVING. Don't talk crazy! My mother would rather fall through the ice . . .
ANNIE. It's in the Chinese food they eat at the Ritz Cafe with the Rosens every Saturday night . . .

IRVING. That's what the brain-damaged, homo Putz, Stanley Rosen said, but, he was just trying to get me in trouble . . .
ANNIE. It's true. It's the little red bits . . .
IRVING. No *wonder* I love the red bits! No *wonder*! God, Annie! How could they just *lie* to me? How could they just look me straight in the eye and lie to me? *How could they?*
ANNIE. They didn't exactly lie . . . It was more like, sort of breaking a law than a lie . . . like driving a little too fast?
IRVING. But they knew it was bacon: they knew they were breaking the law. If you break the law, you break the law. You don't break laws "a little" . . . That's a lot of crap!
ANNIE. Irving!
IRVING. Well, it is! How come they lied to me? How come?
ANNIE. I think we just have to accept the fact that sometimes parents have impossible sets of rules.
IRVING. You mean like with bacon?
ANNIE. Well, yes . . . like with bacon. Or the way my parents are with me . . . and Italians. They think that I should hate all Italians, just because they do . . .
IRVING. Except for the Italians in opera.
ANNIE. (*Suddenly.*) Do you think I should stop seeing Pete? Do you agree with my father?
IRVING. I think you should keep Pete Isanti as your friend. That's what *I* think.
ANNIE. Irving, if you promise not to tell I did it, I'm going to get you a real meal of bacon. More bacon than you've ever seen . . . (*Pauses, then quickly.*) I think that children should have their own sets of rules . . . according to what *they* think is right and wrong, not their parents.
IRVING. What happens if parents find out about certain children having their own certain rules? Won't certain children get their behinds beaten black and blue?
ANNIE. Well, certain parents don't have to ever find out. It is possible for secrets to be kept secret, right?
IRVING. If you will cook me a bacon meal and never tell my parents, I will be your friend for life!
ANNIE. (*In Ukrainian.*) "Te brechaca mene."
IRVING. What does that mean?
ANNIE. That is "Kiss my behind" in Ukrainian.
IRVING. *That's* "Kiss my behind" in Ukrainian? "Te brechaca

mene?" So, what's [Ukrainian words spoken at her arrival.] . . . what I said to you on your first day?
ANNIE. You don't want to know.
IRVING. Oh, God, I do, I really do! (*Annie whispers horrifying obscenity into Irving's ear: a shared private moment. Shocked and thrilled.*) I said that??? (*He faints. Blackout. Lights up in store. Mrs. Ilchak enters. Mrs. Yanover notices her.*)
ESTHER. Can I help you?
MRS. ILCHAK. Hello.
MOSES. (*Realizes.*) You are Annie's Mother! Of course! That face. I know that face . . . Come, come. We'll go upstairs and have some tea. Annie will be delighted . . .
MRS. ILCHAK. (*Frightened.*) No please! I'll see Annie at home next Sunday. (*Mrs. Ilchak produces a large pudding.*)
ESTHER. What's this?
MRS. ILCHAK. This is for you, for your family. We are pleased, Mr. Ilchak and myself, that you took our Annie in your home. We want you to have this, from us.
ESTHER. That is very nice of you . . . (*Looks under cloth cover of bowl at pudding.*) Uh, what is this, exactly?
MRS. ILCHAK. A pudding.
ESTHER. A pudding! How very sweet! Thank you . . .
MOSES. That's very nice of you, Mrs. Ilchak . . .
MRS. ILCHAK. You're both so wonderful to Annie. She tells me things. I thank you both. (*Smiles; nods to pudding.*) I wish it could be more.
ESTHER. Don't be silly. A pudding is wonderful . . .
MOSES. It looks delicious . . .
MRS. ILCHAK. I must go.
ESTHER. Whenever you're in the neighborhood, shopping, please, stop in . . .
MOSES. Please, do . . . (*Mrs. Ilchak smiles, shyly; exits the scene.*) Such a nice face, huh? Just the spitting image of Annie . . .
ESTHER. A pudding yet . . .
MOSES. (*Reaching across for a taste.*) Let me try some . . .
ESTHER. Are you crazy? You would put a Ukranian pudding in your mouth?
MOSES. You can't just throw it out.
ESTHER. I'll give it to Annie. (*Blackout Lights up on Pete, Annie and Irving staring out front, across an imagined Lake Superior, apron of stage.*)

PETE. See those lights — out *there*! That's the United States . . .
ANNIE. It's still called Sault Ste. Marie . . . It's probably not very different from our Sault Ste. Marie . . .
IRVING. Ah, yes, but Sault Ste. Marie, Michigan doesn't have a King in England who quit . . .
PETE. Now, that is true . . .
ANNIE. How did you know that, Irving?
IRVING. I hear. I read . . . My father read a book on King Edward the second that he thought was great, but way too hard for me. He left it in the living room, by accident . . . (*Proudly.*) He was nuts. The book was a cinch. I only had to look up five or six words in the dictionary . . . "Abdicate," "Monarchy," "Despotic," uhnh, "Xenophobe" and a couple of others . . . (*Annie and Pete stare, amazed.*) What are you staring at? (*Blows into his hands.*) How come we're parked here?
ANNIE. No reason.
IRVING. You two wanna' do more smooching?
ANNIE. Irving!
PETE. Yuh.
IRVING. For how long?
PETE. Six minutes worth . . .
IRVING. I'll take a walk . . .
PETE. You will?
IRVING. Yuh, sure . . .
ANNIE. Keep your mittens on.
IRVING. Yuh, sure . . . (*Tightens his coat around him.*) I could die doing this . . . six minutes in the dark forty below zero, wind raging across Lake Superior . . . (*Shrugs.*) . . . buttt, you'll never hear *meee* complain . . . (*Blackout.* * *After a moment, lights up in living room. Moses sits reading the Sunday newspaper; Esther cooks the Sunday meal. The radio plays news from the Front under scene.*)
MOSES. I don't like what I read in my Sunday paper . . . (*Esther looks across; smiles.*)
RADIO ANNOUNCER. (*Under scene.*) The Suez Canal is seriously threatened by a surprise Nazi attack. The first meeting of German and British armies is being fought now on the deserts of North Africa. On these same grounds, the British

*If producing groups wish to have an act break, it should occur here.

forces had their first victory, just last winter, with a three hundred mile mechanized march across Italian Libya, capturing and killing one hundred thousand Italians . . .

MOSES. And I don't like what I hear on my radio, either . . . (*Esther goes to radio, switches it off. She then goes to Moses and takes newspaper from him; kisses him, playfully.*)

ESTHER. Smile, Mosie, it's a nice day, the house is clean, the store is doing well . . . we've got lots to smile about.

MOSES. Is this Esther Yanover I'm hearing?

ESTHER. My spirits are high. It's true. (*Moses sits at dining table. Esther sits on his lap. She smiles seductively.*)

MOSES. (*Suspiciously.*) Well, what's cooking, Esther?

ESTHER. There's nothing cooking . . .

MOSES. Except?

ESTHER. Except I'm feeling good . . . I'm glad that it's sunny out and I think you're a good-looking fellow.

MOSES. Whoa!

ESTHER. "Whoa" is for horses . . .

MOSES. "Hay" is for horses . . . When you tell me I'm a good-looking fellow, I know you've got something important. So *say*!

ESTHER. I was thinking, that since Annie has worked out so well, maybe she should wear a uniform. You know, nothing fancy, just a plain black dress. (*Moses looks up at his wife again, facing her fully.*) And, also, I was thinking that maybe we should get a little apron for her . . . white . . . and maybe a white collar for the little black dress . . . (*Pause. Moses has looked away, pensively.*) Are you listening?

MOSES. I'm listening.

ESTHER. Don't say "no" yet, please.

MOSES. I won't say no.

ESTHER. I was also thinking we could get a little brass bell for the dining room table. It's nicer than calling her. It's not just because Pearl Rosen is doing all these things. It's because it would be like a *promotion* for Annie . . . from live-in-girl to . . . like a live-in- . . . well . . . maid.

MOSES. Is that it?

ESTHER. That's it.

MOSES. Over my dead body! I will *not* have a maid in a uniform in the house and that's *it*!

ESTHER. (*After a pause.*) So, that means "no"?

MOSES. Yes, Esther, that means "no" . . . (*After a long pause.*) Well, am I still a good-looking fellow? (*There is a pause.*)
ESTHER. I've seen better. (*Blackout. Lights up in living room. Moses standing near the door. He holds winter coats, about to go out for the evening. Jive music plays on radio. Annie is drying dishes; sways to the music.*)
MOSES. Esther, it's almost twenty after. We're going to be late . . . (*Irving is at table reading comic book. He sways to music as well.*)
IRVING. Ohh, are you going out, Poppy?
ESTHER. (*Entering, adjusting earring.*) We're going out to eat with the Rosens. You know that. What's the surprise? And why are you not practicing? Did you hear me, Mr. Wax-Gets-In-Your-Ears?
IRVING. In a second I'll practice . . . I promise . . .
ESTHER. I'll promise that when we honk our horn at the Rosens, we'll hear Stanley, upstairs, at the keyboard . . .
IRVING. Yuh, sure. He waits for the honk and then he plays . . .
ESTHER. This Stanley Rosen does not do. Stanley Rosen is dedicated to his piano . . .
IRVING. Stanley Rosen is the only person in life I truly detest . . .
ESTHER. Irving!
MOSES. Irving! (*To Annie, in kitchen doorway.*) You've heard of Hitler? (*Annie nods.*) *Much* nicer than Stanley Rosen . . .
ESTHER. Irving!
MOSES. Irving!
ESTHER. You checked the back door?
MOSES. I checked the back door . . .
ESTHER. You checked the side window?
MOSES. I checked the side windows. A burglar would have to break into this house with a *tank*.
ESTHER. Bite your tongue! (*To Irving.*) Thirty minutes of scales or no "Fibber Magee." (*To Annie.*) And absolutely no "The Shadow Knows" under any circumstance, do you understand?
ANNIE. I would never . . .
ESTHER. I wouldn't want any more nightmares in this house.
ANNIE. I would never.
ESTHER. You hear me Irving Yanover?

IRVING. Don't worry, don't worry.
ESTHER. Kiss your father . . .
MOSES. Kiss your mother . . . (*Esther and Moses kiss Irving; and they exit.*)
ESTHER. Lights out at nine and no talking.
ANNIE. I promise.
IRVING. I promise. Do I have to practice scales?
ESTHER. Young man!
IRVING. Okay, okay . . . (*The Yanovers exit. There is a beat. Irving goes to the window; looks out.*) They're in the car . . . he's starting the engine . . . they're backing out . . . they're *going!* (*Irving runs to the radio, switches station. We hear: "Who know what evil lurks in the hearts of men . . . The Shadow knows . . . "*Annie snaps radio off, and Annie and Irving snap into action. They are preparing a meal of bacon for Irving. Annie lights the stove; Irving runs into the bedroom and runs back into the kitchen carrying a package of bacon, which he tears open. Bacon was hidden outside bedroom window.*)
ANNIE. Careful where you throw the wrapper! No evidence! (*Irving stows wrapper under his bed.*)
IRVING. Oh, God, this is going to be great! This is going to be great! (*Annie puts the strips of bacon on to the skillet. Irving bounces up and down in joyous anticipation. We hear: the sound of bacon frying. Irving bounces enthusiastically.*) Once, I had chocolate-covered orange slices which got me very excited until I ate them. It wasn't chocolate-covered orange slices at all. It was chocolate-covered orange-*peel*, which is disgusting . . . (*Sudden ecstasy.*) Smell it! Smell it! (*Sudden panic.*) It's not burning, is it?
ANNIE. It's fine. It's perfect! Here's the first piece . . . (*She brings a slice of cooked bacon to Irving, dancing around him in tantalizing fashion: cruel master and kindly pup.*)
IRVING. What an odor, Annie! God — You've got to be the best cook in the whole world . . . on the Planet *Earth!* (*Takes a bite; realizes.*) I just burned my mouth, terribly.
ANNIE. I'll get you some water . . .
IRVING. Oh, God, no. Not with bacon! You'll spoil the taste!
ANNIE. You like it?
IRVING. Oh, God, I love it? You know something, Annie?
ANNIE. What?

*See Special Note on copyright page.

IRVING. I have never seen the advantages of growing old as clearly as I do tonight.
ANNIE. What are you talking about?
IRVING. To be able to shop what you want, to be able to cook what you want, to be able to eat what you want: that's worth growing old for . . . (*Smiles.*) Have a smell. Isn't it beautiful?
ANNIE. It's a little heavy . . . Maybe I should open a window?
IRVING. No! I want the smell to linger. Mmmmmmm mmm- mmm. What a treat, Annie, what a treat. Sitting here, Annie, with this smell of perfect bacon in my nostrils, I am very happy, Annie . . . I am a very happy young man . . . (*Suddenly, the sound of door closing in distance; then we hear: footsteps on stairs. Suddenly.*) What's that noise?
ANNIE. *What's what noise?* (*The sound of somebody on the staircase.*)
IRVING. *They're coming back!*
ANNIE. *They're coming back!*
IRVING. They're coming back.
ANNIE. They're coming back. (*Annie and Irving scurry about, trying to wash the pan, clear the plate, etc.*)
IRVING. *Oh, my God!*
ANNIE. *Oh, my God!*
IRVING. *What are we going to do?*
ANNIE. *What are we going to do?* (*They run into the bedroom. Annie throws pan out of window.*)
IRVING. Into bed, into bed!
ANNIE. Into bed! Into bed! (*They leap under covers.*)
IRVING. Go to sleep. Maybe God will be kind! (*Sniff.*) The house smells like a pig. (*There is a pause. Esther enters. She calls out.*)
ESTHER. I'm back. Your father forgot his wallet. Irving, I . . . (*Stops; sniffs.*) It smells like a pig in here . . . (*Realizes.*) Oh, my God . . . (*She turns and runs to the window, yells.*) Mosie, get in here!
IRVING. Oh, God, oh, God, oh, God . . .
ESTHER. Irving Yanoverrrr! Annabell Ilchakkkkkk! Get . . . into . . . this . . . kitchennn . . . immediatelyyyyy! (*Irving pulls the covers from his head, looks at Annie, who pulls the covers from her head. Moses enters the kitchen, from the staircase. He carries pan that Annie threw out of window.*)

MOSES. What? What is this?
ESTHER. Sniff, why don't you?
MOSES. What? (*Sniffs.*) What the hell is that?
ESTHER. Uh huh.
MOSES. Is it?
ESTHER. It certainly is.
MOSES. Irving Yanoverrrr! (*Irving and Annie stand in bedroom doorway.*)
ANNIE. Please, Mrs. Yanover, it was really all my fault . . .
MOSES. Do you know the meaning of the word "trust"? Either of you? Do you?
ANNIE. Please, Mr. Yanover, it's really all my fault. It is really all my fault . . .
ESTHER. Bacon, today; tomorrow, what? *What?* My mother is spinning in her grave . . .
MOSES. *My* mother is spinning in *Toronto*! . . .
ESTHER. I should have known when I first set eyes on you, Annie Ilchak. I should have known! I will have to think about whether you can stay in this house with this family, young lady. I will have to think . . .
MOSES. A boy who is dishonest and untrustworthy to his own mother and father: that's what you are, Irving Yanover. I am going to have to think about this. Now, go to bed . . . (*Yells.*) Both of you! *Quickly!* (*Annie and Irving leap into their beds; terrified. Esther and Moses pace the floor of the bedroom: a chorus of complaint. They complain in unison.*)

MOSES. You know how I hate to lose my temper, you two, but, I have. It's gone. There is a war in Europe and Hitler is doing terrible terrible things to Jewish people. This is no time for you to be untrustworthy. You gave us your word and your word was believed . . . *trusted.* You make me feel foolish for giving you so much trust . . . permission and money for movies, too,

ESTHER. It's not like me to lose my temper, as you well know, but *I am furious!* A "milchadicha" frying pan used for bacon, yet! Bacon! After the lessons I gave you, Annie Ilchak! After the years of upbringing, Irving Yanover. What if the Rosens came in here and sniffed? They would have known? What if your grandmother made a surprise visit What if my own mother

40

movies! You have upset your mother, terribly! Terribly! I'm not complaining for me, but for your mother, Irving. For Mrs. Yanover, Annie. She has given you a great deal of her time and a great deal of her faith . . . her *trust*! I don't care for myself, so much, about these things, but I will not have Mrs. Yanover's feelings hurt! Are you listening? Are you listening? (alivoh, shalom) looked down upon such a scene from Heaven??? It's not for me I'm so angry, but for your father, Irving . . . For Mr. Yanover, Annie! That man trusted you both. That man gave you his That That man gave you money for the movies! Have you even been *going* to the movies? *Hmmmmmm?* Are you listening? Are you listening?

(*They cross through the bedroom a final time, and exit. After a pause, Irving turns on bedlamp. Annie is weeping and Irving is weeping.*)

ANNIE. She's going to fire me, isn't she?
IRVING. She won't. I know she won't.
ANNIE. She fired all the others!
IRVING. My mother never fired anybody. They all quit. My mother would never fire you, Annie.
ANNIE. That's how she sees me: like "Miss Cheese" and the others . . .
IRVING. No, she doesn't!
ANNIE. She does! Irving, she does!
IRVING. How can he call me dishonest when he was on his way to eat bacon at the Ritz Cafe, *himself*? How can he, Annie?
ANNIE. How can my father lie to me about Italian opera?
IRVING. I wasn't going to tell you, but the man who discovered the stars was Italian. We studied him at school. Italians are really great people!
ANNIE. (*Weeps.*) You see? Irving, you see?
IRVING. I think you should see Pete whenever you want and I should eat bacon whenever I want. And that's the truth!
ANNIE. To hell with their goddamn rules!
IRVING. To hell with their goddamn rules! (*Giggles.*) I never heard you swear in English before . . .
ANNIE. I can swear in three different languages . . .
IRVING. English . . . Ukrainian . . .
ANNIE. . . . and Italian . . .
IRVING. Oh, right . . .

ANNIE. "Ah bah fah Napola!"
IRVING. What's that?
ANNIE. "Go to Hell" in Italian . . .
IRVING. (*Giggles.*) That is so nifty! (*Suddenly.*) You know something Annie? You could bring Pete here, to my parents' house, to visit and all . . .
ANNIE. Oh, noooo . . .
IRVING. But, you could. They've no rules against Italians here . . .
ANNIE. I would never dare . . . But, you know something, Irving? I could take you to my house for a totally legal bacon meal. You could come home with me some Sunday . . . if you dare . . .
IRVING. If I dare? Are you kidding? I dare . . . You're a genius, Annie. (*Pauses thoughtfully.*) You know something, Annie. I'm going to stop talking to my parents. I'm never going to talk to them again, not until they tell me why they can eat bacon and I can't . . . (*Irving moves into living room. Lights shift with him. Esther and Moses stand at kitchen door, worried, smiling. Irving walks silently past them.*)
MOSES. You're going to school? (*Irving gets his coat, wordlessly.*) You're still not talking? (*Irving puts on his cap; mittens, arranges his bookbag. Esther offers a polished, red apple.*)
ESTHER. Would you like to take an apple, for later? (*Irving is tempted. He silently fetches the apple.*) You're still not talking? (*Irving calls across the house — and across his parents — to Annie.*)
IRVING. I'm off for school. Bye, Annie . . .
ANNIE. (*Calls from bedroom.*) Bye, Irving . . . (*Irving exits the house, out front door, slamming same. There is a pause. Esther and Moses turn, at the same time, look at one another.*)
ESTHER. He's still not talking.
MOSES. He's still not talking. (*Annie exits bedroom, crosses into kitchen. Moses is at* L. *of kitchen door.*) Irving's just left for school . . .
ESTHER. (R. *of kitchen door.*) We'll be going down to the shop to open up . . . (*Annie passes them, wordlessly, shoving them aside. She begins washing Irving's breakfast dishes in kitchen. To Moses; a whisper.*) She's still not talking, either . . .
MOSES. She's still not talking, either . . . (*Lights shift to store. Irving enters, starts stacking boxes. Moses calls across to him and moves to*

store; enters.) It's very nice of you to help out in the store; even though you're not talking . . . (*Irving continues to stack boxes, wordlessly. Moses crosses to Esther, who sits at table. Esther is reading a book*) He still won't talk to me.
ESTHER. (*Not looking up.*) He will, sooner or later.
MOSES. Why do you say that?
ESTHER. (*Not looking up.*) Because he will . . .
MOSES. How do you know that?
ESTHER. Because it stands to reason . . .
MCSES. Well, it's almost a week now . . .
ESTHER. You think I don't know that?
MOSES. It doesn't seem to upset you . . .
ESTHER. You didn't notice my book is upside down? (*He turns her book right-side-up.*)
MOSES. I noticed . . . (*Sighs.*) It's really quite simple. He knows we've lied to him. He knows we have a double standard. He knows we've punished him severely for something we do ourselves . . .
ESTHER. (*Taps table with fingernail ends, for emphasis.*) But not in the house!
MOSES. That's a pretty complicated notion for a ten-year-old. Now that I think about it, it's a pretty complicated notion for a forty-one-year-old . . .
ESTHER. You're forty-two . . .
MOSES. (*Slaps hand down on tabletop, in disgust.*) Please, don't do that!
ESTHER. So? What do you suggest? You're the man. I'm just the woman . . .
MOSES. That is so *annoying* when you do that! (*Mr. Ardenshensky "knocks on door" to store. He is extremely old. He carries a brown paper bag. He is drenched from the rain.*)
ARDENSHENSKY. (*Offstage.*) Yanover? Are you here or are you closed? (*Moses calls down from front window.*)
MOSES. It's a little late. Who is that?
ARDENSHENSKY. Ardenshensky. It's freezing down here. There is ice on my eyebrows!
MOSES. (*To Esther.*) It's old Ardenshensky . . . (*To Ardenshensky.*) I'll be right down, Ardenshensky . . .
ESTHER. Good. We can talk to Ardenshensky. He knows

everything. You keep him amused till I get there. I'll make some tea. (*Lights shift as Moses crosses to shop. Jacob Ardenshensky enters, dripping wet.*)

MOSES. Here, Ardenshensky, wipe off with this towel . . .

ARDENSHENSKY. I should wipe off with new merchandise?

MOSES. It's last year's model. You shouldn't worry, Ardenshensky. You'll catch your death. Wipe . . .

ARDENSHENSKY. A man of my age doesn't *catch* his death. Death, to a man of my age, is an easy grounder. You just fall on it.

MOSES. What are you talking about, Ardenshensky?

ARDENSHENSKY. Baseball, Yanover, baseball . . .

MOSES. What do you know from baseball? A man like you . . .

ARDENSHENSKY. What do you know from death? A man like *you*.

MOSES. What brings you out in a storm?

ARDENSHENSKY. I ripped my sheet.

MOSES. You only have one?

ARDENSHENSKY. How many should I have? *I'm* not in the sheet business, you are . . .

MOSES. Was it defective?

ARDENSHENSKY. Possibly.

MOSES. Are you sure that you bought it from me, Ardenshensky. I haven't seen you in the store for twenty years . . .

ARDENSHENSKY. (*Slams bag down on countertop.*) That's the sheet!

MOSES. That's the sheet?

ARDENSHENSKY. It ripped. Sarah was making our bed and it ripped. About fifteen minutes ago. I fired right on over here. (*Displays sheet, in brown paper bag. Yanover holds back a laugh.*)

MOSES. What can I do for you? I'll be happy to give you a refund . . .

ARDENSHENSKY. Did I say anything about a refund?

MOSES. What can I do for you?

ARDENSHENSKY. I'm back in the market.

MOSES. (*Smiles.*) Oh. I have here a sheet that is fortified with pure nylon. This sheet's guaranteed for thirty years or double your money back . . . this sheet is built for hard use . . .

ARDENSHENSKY. I'm seventy-seven years old, Yanover. What kind of "hard use" are you talking? In thirty years, I won't

be needing double my money, I'll be needing a *miracle!* How much?
MOSES. Forget it, ... it's a gift.
ARDENSHENSKY.   Is this life, Yanover, if you *take* a gift, you have to *give a* gift. I would prefer not to get involved, thank you. What's your best price?...
MOSES. For this sheet? Six dollars.
ARDENSHENSKY. A first price is never a best price.
MOSES. *(Laughs lovingly.)* Ah, but for you, Ardenshensky, I started right at the bottom.... But I can go lower. Make me an offer ...
ARDENSHENSKY. There is a philosophical-Talmudical question afoot here, Yanover: should a man of seventy-seven get involved with a sheet that is designed for thirty years? Or have you got something that is, maybe, one-sixth as good — that will last one-sixth the time and cost one-sixth the price?
MOSES. A *dollar?*
ARDENSHENSKY. I'm not a rich man, Yanover ...
MOSES. Cash or charge ...
ARDENSHENSKY.   Charge is "Goyim-nachas." Jacob Ardenshensky pays cash ...
MOSES. One dollar, cash ... *(Esther enters, hands him a glass of tea.)*
ESTHER. Good to see you, Mister Ardenshensky ...
ARDENSHENSKY.   *(Smiles at Esther.)* You look very well, Mrs. Yanover ...
ESTHER.   Thank you. You're looking very well yourself, Mr. Ardenshensky. You also look drenched. Here, dry off ... *(Passes a towel to Ardenshensky.)*
ARDENSHENSKY. No, I'm dry as a bone already.
ESTHER. No, no. Just in case ... wipe your hair again. It couldn't hurt ...
ARDENSHENSKY. For you, I'll do it. I don't know how you've made a living, the way you both waste new towels ... and your husband's letting sheets go way below cost ...
ESTHER. Well, easy come, easy go, Mr. Ardenshensky. And how is Mrs. Ardenshensky? Anything new?
ARDENSHENSKY. Very little beyond this sheet, Mrs. Yanover ...
MOSES. We sold him inferior goods ... many years ago ...
ARDENSHENSKY. Anything new with you, Mrs. Yanover?

ESTHER. Well, Mr. Ardenshensky, I'm glad you should ask, I think we're having a little trouble with our Irving . . .
ARDENSHENSKY. Schoolwork?
ESTHER. Bacon.
MOSES. Irving insists on eating bacon . . .
ARDENSHENSKY. A Jewish boy insists on eating bacon?
ESTHER and MOSES. (*In unison; in shame.*) I know . . . I know . . .
ARDENSHENSKY. So, tell him not to . . .
MOSES. Jacob, it's a mess . . .
ESTHER. We lied to our son . . .
MOSES. Esther!
ESTHER. Well, it's true, we did. He wanted to eat bacon and we told him that Jews don't, but, he found out we do . . . in the fried rice and the egg foo yong at the Ritz Cafe . . .
ARDENSHENSKY. Oh, the Ritz Cafe. Nothing but "traif," the worst . . .
MOSES. Nevertheless, we all eat there . . .
ARDENSHENSKY. (*In shame.*) I know, I know . . .
ESTHER. He found out . . .
ARDENSHENSKY. Well, really, I mean, this is 1941 . . . It's not so terrible, really, I mean really, it's only in the egg foo yong and the fried rice . . .
MOSES. We know it's not so terrible, but children have other ideas.
ARDENSHENSKY. Oh, well, children . . .
MOSES. That' not the worst.
ARDENSHENSKY. Oh. Tell me the worst.
MOSES. He and the live-in girl did it together . . .
ARDENSHENSKY. *What?*
ESTHER. We caught them . . .
MOSES. We came home early . . .
ESTHER. Mosie forgot his wallet . . . we turned around . . .
MOSES. We caught them at it . . .
ESTHER. In the kitchen . . .
ARDENSHENSKY. In the kitchen?
MOSES. They ran into the bedroom . . .
ARDENSHENSKY. How old is the girl?
ESTHER. Fifteen . . .
ARDENSHENSKY. And your son?

MOSES. Ten and a half . . .
ARDENSHENSKY. Ten and a half years old? That's all?
ESTHER. He's bright for his age . . .
ARDENSHENSKY. Doing it? In the kitchen? With the live-in girl?
ESTHER. Cooking bacon, Mister Ardenshensky, cooking bacon!
ARDENSHENSKY. Cooking bacon?
MOSES. What the hell did you think we were telling you?
ARDENSHENSKY. I'm not sure . . .
ESTHER. The house was full of smoke . . .
MOSES. It smelled like a pig in there . . .
ARDENSHENSKY. So, what did you do?
MOSES. We punished them.
ESTHER. We threatened terrible things and we punished them . . .
ARDENSHENSKY. Was it before or after the Ritz Cafe information reached him? . . .
MOSES. After. But he must have known before. That's why he probably felt free to cook the bacon . . .
ESTHER. He's stopped talking . . .
MOSES. Her, too . . .
ESTHER. Both of them . . .
ARDENSHENSKY. Not a word?
MOSES. A few words . . .
ESTHER. It's been nearly a week.
ARDENSHENSKY. Well, getting children to keep strictly Kosher in this day and age . . . I don't know . . . Things are changing, Yanover. My own grandson ate a porkchop and my son, Allen, took a strap to him. It was exactly the same thing. My Allen is a shellfish eater. The boy knew . . . (*Pauses.*) I'll tell you what I told Allen . . . (*Moses enters.*)
MOSES. Please, Mr. Ardenshensky, I'm desperate. My son won't talk to me . . .
ARDENSHENSKY. I told Allen "Being Jewish is bigger than a porkchop . . ."
MOSES. (*After a long pause.*) I see what you mean, Mr. Ardenshensky. Thank you very much, Mr. Ardenshensky, thank you.
ARDENSHENSKY. So, you'll let me exchange this sheet? (*He

holds up paper bag.)
MOSES. Keep the nylon-fortified and take two more from the same range. It's not a gift, it's an even exchange. A good piece of advice is well worth three sheets . . . (*Laughs, waves sheets away.*)
ARDENSHENSKY. Very very generous. When your husband opened this store, I said to my wife "Yanover is a fine boy. He'll go far." Luckily, you're still young and there's still time . . .
ESTHER. (*Into intercom.*) Don't either of you move! We're coming right up! (*Lights shift to Annie and Irving in living room, frightened.*)
IRVING. Be tough, Annie. You know what it says in the newspaper: "War Is Hell" . . .
ANNIE. Just don't you start being a wiseacre!
IRVING. *Me?* Oh, God, here they come! (*Esther and Moses enter the living room. Irving and Annie move silently about the room, pretending to busy themselves in activity: Annie dusts, Irving stacks his piano scores, etc. Esther starts to speak; loses her courage.*)
ESTHER. Your father will speak for both of us.
MOSES. (*Amazed; looks at Esther who shrugs; looks at Irving; speaks.*) There have been certain misunderstandings that want to be cleared up. You mother and I are sure that you and Annie are both sorry that you cooked bacon in this house; and your mother and I are both sorry that we lost our tempers. We love you both and we want you to talk. We would like life to continue as normal. If you will accept *our apology*, we will accept yours. (*There is a silence.*)
ANNIE. I accept. Thank you. (*Irving is silent; Annie yells at him.*) Irving!
IRVING. (*Talks for the first time in a week.*) Okay. It's a deal. But, on one condition. (*Esther and Moses exchange a smile. Irving and Annie exchange a smile.*) On Sunday, when Annie goes home for dinner with her family, she was thinking it might be fun for me to come along for the visit with her . . . since you two are always pushing me towards trying new things and I've never been in Annie's house before . . .
MOSES. That sounds like a great idea. We could drive you ourselves when we go over to eat with the Rosens . . .
ESTHER. We're going to their house! Not to the Ritz Cafe.
MOSES. Right . . . Have you checked with Annie?

IRVING. Uh would it be alright with you if I came along with you on Sunday? To your parents' house to visit and all?
ANNIE. Sure, that'd be great. My parents are dying to meet you . . .
ESTHER. And how about *my* permission?
IRVING. Are you giving permission?
ESTHER. Only if you're giving kisses . . .
IRVING. Blackmail?
ESTHER. Precisely . . .
IRVING. Then I've got no choice . . . (*He kisses his mother; giggles.*) How come you eat bacon in restaurants and then punish me for eating it at home? (*There is a small silence.*)
ESTHER. Ask your father.
IRVING. Poppy, how come you yourself eat bacon in restaurants and then you . . .
MOSES. (*Interrupting.*) I heard the question.
IRVING. You like me to keep talking?
MOSES. Is this what I think it is?
IRVING. Precisely.
MOSES. (*Sighs.*) Go get your coat. We're taking a walk. The subject for tonight's walk is "The Double Standard" . . . Get my coat and your coat. (*Annie smiles. Irving runs for the coats. Esther looks at her husband; smiles happily.*)
ESTHER. He's talking. (*Moses starts to talk, thinks better of it; shrugs. Irving hands him his coat, which he puts on.*)
MOSES. Forty-below-zero and I'm stepping outside to tell my son I can't be trusted. (*To Irving.*) You ready?
IRVING. Let's hit it. (*Music: Chopin. Irving and Moses exit. Annie crosses to Pete, opposite side of stage. Irving joins them. Light shift during move. Irving talks to Pete and Annie, chirping enthusiastically. Annie seems depressed, secretive, mysterious.*) This is the most nifty weekend of my life, really . . . Us all going to the movies today, and Annie and I going to her parents' tomorrow for you-know-what. No work in the store, but I still get my dollar-fifty . . . (*Realizes Pete and Annie are depressed.*) What's with you two? Something wrong?
PETE. I think you'd better go to the movies without us, Irving . . .
IRVING. How come?
PETE. Annie and I have got a lot to talk about . . .

49

IRVING. We can skip the movies. We can just go someplace else, where talking's okay . . .
PETE. We want to talk alone, Irving . . .
IRVING. Without me?
PETE. Yuh.
IRVING. How come? Did I do something wrong?
PETE. Uh uh . . . We just have to talk . . . All right?
IRVING. (*Sees that Annie is weeping.*) Is Annie crying?
PETE. No . . . Annie is not crying.
ANNIE. I'm not crying, Irving. Pete and I just have to talk about something. You go in. We'll be waiting right here on the sidewalk as soon as the movie's over . . .
IRVING. I don't wanna' go in alone . . .
ANNIE. Please, Irving . . .
IRVING. (*Sternly.*) I don't think that Annie should be unhappy, Pete . . .
ANNIE. I'm not unhappy, Irving. Thank you for worrying, but I'm really fine. Really. Please, go in . . .
IRVING. I don't like this . . . (*He backs toward movie theatre, away from Pete and Annie.*)
ANNIE. Thanks, Irving . . .
PETE. Thanks, kid . . .
IRVING. I really hate this . . . Tomorrow's still on, right?
ANNIE. Of course, Irving . . .
IRVING. It better be . . . (*Irving is about to cry. Instead, he turns and runs away from Annie and Pete. He runs to his bed, hops under the covers. Lights shift with him. Annie goes to her bed, gets under covers. Pete exits. There is a moment's pause. In the darkness we hear Irving's voice; whispered.*) Annie?
ANNIE. What?
IRVING. You mad at me or something?
ANNIE. No, 'course not! (*Irving turns on the bedlamp. Lights up in bedroom, Irving leans across from his bed to Annie, who lies atop her bed, wide awake.*)
IRVING. What's the matter?
ANNIE. I'm just nervous about going to my parents' house . . . tomorrow.
IRVING. You shouldn't be nervous. It's totally legal. No bacon in *this* house. Eating bacon at your parents' house isn't in *this* house, so . . .

ANNIE. That's not it, Irving. It's something else . . .
IRVING. Are you and Pete fighting with each other?
ANNIE. Pete and I have some really big news that is making us both really nervous . . .
IRVING. Oh, *great*! Did he get picked by the Red Wings?
ANNIE. Irving, this is the deepest darkest secret I've ever told you, so you better not even breathe a *hint*, okay?
IRVING. Sure, Annie, sure! What is it?
ANNIE. Pete and I are getting married, very very soon . . .
IRVING. Very very *sooon*? Why, Annie, *why*?
ANNIE. Irving, for *some* things, you're just really too young, okay? (*Annie leans back on her bed, hands behind her head, worried. Irving leans back on his bed; heartbroken; betrayed. He turns away from Annie; faces front. He stands, crosses to piano. Lights crossfade to living room. Music in, immediately. The sound of Irving practicing Chopin, on tape. Esther and Moses enter, exhausted, in bathrobes.*)
ESTHER. (*Calls out to Irving.*) So early you're practicing?
MOSES. (*Calls out to Irving.*) So early you're practicing?
ESTHER. (*Looks at clock.*) It's only six a.m. and on a Sunday morning! (*Irving is crying. He pounds his fists down on keyboard.*)
IRVING. I'll stop, okay? (*Pound.*) Okay, okay . . . (*Pound.*) I'll stop . . . (*Pound.*) Okay? Okay . . . (*Irving puts his head down on the keyboard. He tries to stop his sobbing. Esther and Moses listen; look at one another. Esther calls out.*)
ESTHER. What's with you? (*To Moses.*) What's with him? (*The lights fade out. Music in, immediately. On tape, we hear Caruso, singing an aria from "Rigoletto." The lights fade up on the dining area and kitchen. We are now in the Ilchak home. Annie's father, Emil Ilchak, sits looking at Irving and Annie. Annie's mother works at the stove, upstage. The music is quite prominent and Ilchak takes delight in it.*)
ILCHAK. So, this is the little Jew-boy they never let eat pork, eh? Well, today's going to be your big day . . .
IRVING. It's bacon that I like. Pork I don't think I like so much.
ILCHAK. You like Caruso? I hear you like music.
IRVING. I *love* music. I have a Caruso record like this . . . "La donna è mobile" from "Rigoletta," right?
ILCHAK. (*To all, smiling.*) He's a very smart young man, this one . . .
ANNIE. I've been learning a great deal about music, too, papa

. . . Caruso is Italian and so is the man who wrote "Rigoletto." I'm starting to think that all the really *great* opera composers and opera singers are Italian, don't you, Papa?
ILCHAK. Some Italians write good music, and some sing good, too . . . (*He stands, turns off record. Music stops. He calls to his wife.*) Let's get this meal, huh? Who's got all day to wait?
MRS. ILCHAK. (*In Ukrainian.*) Who the hell do you think you're talking to that way, huh?
ILCHAK. (*In Ukrainian.*) You're taking all day. I've got work to do, right? The kid's got to get home, too . . .
MRS. ILCHAK. (*In Ukrainian.*) I'm getting it now!
IRVING. (*Frightened.*) Maybe you went too far?
ANNIE. It's nothing. They're always like this . . .
MRS. ILCHAK. (*To Irving; in Ukrainian.*) I'll bring your food right away. I'm sorry there's this confusion. Cooking two meals . . . we ate already, ourselves . . .
IRVING. (*Panicked.*) What did she say to me?
ANNIE. She said your bacon's coming. Whenever she gets nervous, she forgets how to speak English. She's nervous now . . .
ILCHAK. (*Smiling.*) We ate our meal already. This is special for Annie's friend, yes? (*Mrs. Ilchak puts a platter with cooked bacon strips on table.*)
MRS. ILCHAK. Hot.
ILCHAK. A whole week's supply, huh?
IRVING. Oh, God, it's beautiful . . .
ILCHAK. Good bacon? You like?
IRVING. This is the very best bacon I've ever eaten in my entire life! Oh, God, it's great! (*Irving chomps and chatters. Everyone watches and listens.*) I've only had bacon four times in my life before this. Once at Freddy Folger's, my friend's . . . Twice at the Ritz Cafe, but that was just little red bits in soupy sauce and stuff . . . Once for real at home, but we don't talk about that, do we, Annie? . . . (*Annie laughs.*) This, I can safely say, is my very favorite meal. Well, almost my favorite. Maybe tied. Lately. I have been loving spaghetti almost as much as bacon. Annie's boyfriend takes me for spaghetti all the time. He's going to take me to a place where they sell spaghetti with bacon and an egg right on top of it . . .
ILCHAK. (*Stunned.*) *Which* boyfriend?
IRVING. (*Terrified to do what he is about to do.*) Pete Lisanti.

ANNIE. (*Horrified.*) Irving! (*Irving stands; runs from the table and into his bedroom. He leaps into bed and hides under the covers, out of sight.*)
ILCHAK. (*In Ukrainian.*) You lied to me! You lied to me! (*Annie runs D.: outside. Her mother follows. Annie is sobbing.*)
MRS. ILCHAK. (*In Ukrainian.*) Let me look at your face. Look at me . . .
ANNIE. (*Faces her mother.*) It's too late, mama . . . (*Annie runs from D. up, through the dining area, to the other bedroom. The lights crossfade to bedroom. Annie sits on bed, faces the lump on the other bed that is Irving, hiding. The bedlamp is on. It is night. They are home at the Yanovers'.*) Why?! (*No reply.*) I know you're awake, Irving. I want to know why. I *deserve* to know why. You gave me your sacred word. (*No reply.*) You could start crying now if you want . . . or you could be a decent human being and tell me why you betrayed me . . . (*No response.*) Irving? (*Irving, without lifting his head from his pillow, he answers: staring off to the wall, weeping; frightened and ashamed.*)
IRVING. I always thought you were kidding when you said you and Pete were getting married. When you told me you were really going to do it . . . I . . . I wanted to stop it, I guess . . .
ANNIE. Irving, pay attention. I am pregnant and Pete and I are getting married, okay?
IRVING. Okay.
ANNIE. So, that's clear to you?
IRVING. Yes.
ANNIE. So, there you go.
IRVING. If you marry him you'll never get out of Sault Ste. Marie . . . Pete's not going to be a Detroit Red Wing, Annie. He's not good enough . . .
ANNIE. Maybe I don't want to . . . get out of Sault Ste. Marie!
IRVING. (*Sits up, sharply, amazed.*) Annie!
ANNIE. I like it. It's my home.
IRVING. Everybody good in Sault Ste. Marie has to leave. You have to go to Montreal . . . Toronto . . . New York . . . The world, Annie. You're going to be *famous*! You can't stay here!
ANNIE. Pete Lisanti is a good hockey player . . . only good. I know that. But he's going to be a good husband, too, Irving. He never lies. He'll never drink: he promised me that and I believe

him. He'll never go off with other women . . . He's honest and strong and handsome and he loves children . . .
IRVING. He'll never have money . . .
ANNIE. We'll have enough. We're not Jewish, you know, I mean it's not like we're going to need two sets of dishes and two sets of silverware, right? (*She leans closer to Irving.*) I'm never going to be famous, Irving . . . never. I'm Annie Ilchak from Bayview. I want a clean house and a nice husband and a small family: two children at the most. *They* can leave Sault Ste. Marie. I don't want to. (*Pauses: softly.*) You can. I have no reason.
IRVING. There was the other Ukrainian girl: she left. And Roseanne, the half-Italian: she left . . . and the other Annie, too. They *all* left! You can't leave me, too, Annie! Please stay!
ANNIE. I won't ever be far away, Irving. If you ever need to talk, I won't be far away . . . (*Does not finish . . . Irving buries his head in his pillow, sobbing. Lights crossfade* D., *to Emil Ilchak, wearing heavy mackinaw. He faces Pete Lisanti, who wears a tweed coat; team scarf.*)
PETE. I love Annie, Mr. Ilchak. I'll be a good husband. I swear this to you . . .
ILCHAK. Why shouldn't I just break your neck?
PETE. You'll see. I'll take care of Annie. I'll be a good husband. I swear it to you . . .
ILCHAK. Emil Ilchak will have an eye on you, believe me . . .
PETE. Mr. Ilchak, Annie and I are getting married no matter what. You and I can be friends, or it could go the other way. That decision is yours . . . but, Annie and I *are* getting married . . . and it's not because we *have* to, it's because we *want* to.
ILCHAK. What are you? Nineteen? (*Pete nods.*) You think at nineteen you know what you want?
PETE. Didn't you?
ILCHAK. When I was nineteen, I had one baby already and another one coming. I knew nothing.
PETE. Are you sorry?
ILCHAK. I'm sorry that I'm forty and I look fifty and I feel a hundred! I'm sorry that there never was one single week in twenty years when I really and truly knew I was going to earn enough money to put enough food on the table . . . or to pay off

the loan payments on a house that's too small and too ugly to be worth a man's life of work . . .
PETE. Annie and I are only going to have two children. One next year and the other one in two more years . . . after we have the down-payment on a house.
ILCHAK. I see.
PETE. Mr. Ilchak, you're going to be really proud of both of us.
ILCHAK. What about your hockey?
PETE. (*After a pause.*) I can play . . . sometimes. I can make a little extra money at it too, you know. Last week, we split a purse of nearly thirty dollars . . . two dollars a man.
ILCHAK. Two dollars buy peanuts when you have a family.
PETE. *Extra* peanuts . . . for a small family. (*Ilchak studies Pete's face a moment.*)
ILCHAK. I warn you, Lisanti . . . no funny business while I'm alive. And after I'm dead, I'll *still* be looking over your shoulder.
PETE. I swear to you, Mr. Ilchak: no funny business.
ILCHAK. (*Sharply.*) You like opera? (*Pete shows his palms, shakes them, making a "so-so" comment. Ilchak is disgusted, rolls his eyes to heaven in a "why me" gesture. Lights widen, suddenly: The entire stage brightens. Irving plays start of "The Wedding March" on piano. Annie enters,* D.R., *in a simple white wedding dress, with her mother and an elderly Ukrainian priest (Ardenshensky); joined by Pete, and Ilchak, in ill-fitting suits; (pre-dressed under mackinaws). They all form a wedding tableau. They stand frozen in place,* D.L. *As soon as they are in position, Irving stops playing, bangs his hand down on the piano. With the bang, a light switches on in piano area. Light remains on as well,* D.)
IRVING. I'm not going! I'm not going! (*Esther pops her head out of bedroom; she is dressing: fancy dress-up dress and hat.*)
ESTHER. What's this?
IRVING. (*Ripping off necktie. Throws same on floor.*) I'm not going!
ESTHER. That is a pure silk tie that costs two dollars and fifty cents, young man!
IRVING. (*Picks it up.*) This cost two fifty?
ESTHER. Cash.
IRVING. I'm *still* not going!
ESTHER. (*Calls out.*) Mosie!

MOSES. (*Enters from bedroom, tying his tie.*) I heard. (*To Irving.*) It took me ten minutes to tie that thing. Why'd you take it off?
ESTHER. He's not going.
MOSES. What does this mean?
IRVING. I'm not going. What could "I'm not going" mean? It means *I'm not going!*
MOSES. Why aren't you going?
IRVING. Why is Annie marrying Pete? *Really*, why?
ESTHER. Well, Irving, that's . . .
MOSES. That's quite a complicated question . . .
IRVING. What's complicated about it? Why is Annie marrying Pete Lisanti? Really?
ESTHER. Well, Irving, it's commmplicateddd beecaussee . . .
MOSES. (*Interrupting.*) Annie is pregnant. That's one of the major major major reasons she's marrying Pete Lisanti. She is pregnant.
IRVING. I know *that.*
ESTHER. You know that?
MOSES. You know that?
IRVING. I know that.
MOSES. So, why are you making us stand here, embarrassed, blushing, sweating . . . ?
IRVING. By why doesn't Annie's father stop it?
MOSES. The wedding?
IRVING. The being pregnant. I understand that a pregnant woman should get married, but, it Mr. Ilchak hates Pete so much, why doesn't he simply insist that Annie stop being pregnant?
ESTHER. I seee. Mr. Know-It-All is really Mr. *Almost*-Know-It-All . . .
IRVING. I know a lot!
ESTHER. So, listen, and you'll know a little more. When a woman is pregnant, she stays pregnant . . . for nine months, no matter what . . . until the baby is born . . .
IRVING. (*Shocked.*) *Baby*? What baby? What baby, Mama? (*An angel flies by the window: there is a pause.*)
ESTHER. Mosie!
MOSES. Irving, supposing you and I bundle up and walk to the wedding, just the two of us . . . two fellas . . . We should talk about this. Your mother will drive the car and meet us there . . .

IRVING. If you think.
MOSES. I think.
ESTHER. I'll get your coat. You don't want to miss the whole wedding ceremony . . . (*Esther turns* U.; *goes to Irving's jacket on hook.*)
IRVING. Did Chopin have a wife, Poppy?
MOSES. Ask me outside. I'll tell you.
IRVING. Promise?
MOSES. I promise . . .
IRVING. A promise is a promise . . .
MOSES. Take your necktie. We'll tie it on the road . . .
IRVING. Papa, why do men wear neckties, anyway?
MOSES. I don't know why men wear neckties, Irving. I really don't. Neckties neither keep your neck warm nor comfortable. They are silly-looking, a waste of time to tie and get ruined by soup. Furthermore, they are expensive.
IRVING. How come you wear a necktie then?
MOSES. Because my father did. And his father before him. I never broke the family habit. If you would like to, be my guest. You could be the first Yanover man to never wear a necktie. (*Pauses.*) There are many things about this family you have the power to change . . . believe-you-me.
IRVING. Maybe I'll keep it in my pocket . . . just in case . . . (*He puts necktie in his pocket.*)
MOSES. Remember the story I told you about my cousin Quentin?
IRVING. The schmuck with all the fountain pens?
MOSES. (*Winces at word "schmuck."*) Shhh, your mother . . .
ESTHER. (*Shocked.*) What's this?
MOSES. (*Teams with Irving.*) Man's talk . . .
IRVING. (*Giggles.*) Two fellas . . . (*Moses kneels, buttons Irving's coat; hugs Irving.*)
MOSES. Quentin was thirteen and, I'll tell you the truth, he was *not* a fountain pen. But, you, Irving, at ten years old, you are really and truly a fountain pen . . .
IRVING. I am? (*Esther looks out front, to audience.*)
ESTHER. This genius he gets from my side of the family . . .
(*The Wedding March plays enthusiastically, on tape. Pete and Annie kiss. Esther and Moses embrace Irving. Ilchak and Mrs. Ilchak hug each other; the priest smiles. The lights fade to black. As soon as audience ap-*

plauds, lights to full. The actors bow once, then, suddenly Ardenshensky, who is, of course, costumed as the Ukrainian priest, holds up a hand; talks to audience, confidentially.)

ARDENSHENSKY. It's me: Ardenshensky . . . (*Lifts off headdress.*) You thought maybe I was a Ukrainian Priest? (*Smiles.*) I'm an actor. I'm working . . . (*Looks at watch.*) See? It didn't take so long, this play? It's only [time of day] . . . (*Smiles.*) I should leap ahead a little and tell you what became of some of us . . . (*Looks at Annie.*) Annie and Pete had a boy who they named Enrico Irving Lisanti . . . Enrico for Caruso, and Irving for the fountain pen . . . Five years later they had a daughter, Elsa Esther Lisanti. Pete quit Algoma Steel and opened a sporting goods store on Queen Street which he and Annie co-managed. According to Annie, it did "a nice business." . . . Emil Ilchak died from silicosis at age fifty-two, but was extremely close to his son-in-law Pete, and taught his grandson Enrico to sing the first two choruses of "La donna è mobile" . . . in Italian. Else Ilchak moved in with Annie and Pete and lived to the ripe old age of eighty-one . . . As for Irving and Esther and Mosie Yanover, they have two more plays to go . . . "A Rosen by Any Other Name," starring none other than Irving's dearest enemy, Stanley Rosen; and "The Chopin Playoffs," starring three Yanovers, three Rosens and two Steinways . . . (*Smiles.*) As for me, Jacob Ardenshensky, I never lived so I never died. I'm just a character in a play with a very happy ending. (*Wedding music plays to conclusion. The lights fade to black.*)

THE PLAY IS OVER

NOTE: "Today, I Am A Fountain Pen" is the first play in a trilogy, "Growing Up Jewish." The remaining plays, "A Rosen By Any Other Name" and "The Chopin Playoffs," have also been published by Dramatists Play Service.

PROPERTY LIST

Onstage

Piano (old-fashioned, upright)
Oversized dining table
Intercom (homemade; funnel-mouthpiece at each end of a tube; 2 smallish bells, spring-mounted, joined by lightweight chainlink)
Chicken
Comic book
Smoldering pot-holder
Pot
Stoves
Chairs
Newspaper
Sewing
Tea
Cake
Bed
Dresser
Annie's things
Dilapidated suitcase
Twine
Telephone
Dishtowel
Pencil
Paper
Bedlamp
Iron
Shirts
Clock
Boxes of fresh, new merchandise
Winter coats
Radio
Package of bacon
Skillet
Slice of cooked bacon
Plate

Apple (polished, red)
Breakfast dishes
Book
Towels (2)
Sheets
Platter of cooked bacon strips
Neckties
Jacket

Offstage

Glass of tea (Annie)
Biscuit (Annie)
Money (Pete)
Box of popcorn (Irving)
Scarf (Pete)
Armload of boxes (Irving)
Pudding (cloth-covered bowl) (Mrs. Ilchak)
Earring (Esther)
Brown paper bag (with sheet inside) (Ardenshensky)
Glass of tea (Esther)
Heavy mackinaw (Ilchak)
Tweed coat (Pete)
Team scarf (Pete)
Watch (Ardenshensky)

COSTUME PLOT
(Prepared by Mimi Maxmen)

ESTHER YANOVER

Dress
Apron
Shoes
Hose
Girdle
Rings
Watch
Earrings
Slip

Bathrobe
Slippers

Cardigan sweater
Coat
Hat

Wedding dress
Shoes
Hat
Handbag
Gloves
Earrings
Bracelet
Necklace

ANNIE ILCHAK

Skirt
Sweater
Undershirt
Cardigan
Shoes
Anklets
Mittens
Scarf

Hat
Purse
Coat
Necklace
Apron

Wedding dress
Hat/veil
Hose
Garter belt
Shoes
Gloves
Slip
Earrings
Necklace

MRS. ILCHAK

Housedress
Shoes
Garter belt
Hose
Apron
Wedding band
Slip
Cardigan

Coat
Babushka
Gloves
Neck scarf
Pocketbook

Wedding dress
Hat
Gloves
Shoes
Corsage
Necklace
Earrings

IRVING YANOVER

Knickers
Sweater
Belt
High sox
High lace shoes
Coat/jacket
Scarf
Mittens
Hat

2 piece navy, Norfolk knicker suit
White, 1-s shirt
Tie
High sox
Belt

MOSES YANOVER

3 piece brown suit
Blue shirt
White shirt
2 ties
Suspenders
Shoes
Sox
Watch
Cufflinks
Shop jacket
Wedding band

Bathrobe
Slippers
Pajamas

Coat
Hat
Gloves
Scarf

2 piece/d.b. blue wedding suit
Tie
Suspenders
Sox

PETE LISANTI

Hockey jersey
Corduroy pants
Belt
Sox
Athletic shoes
Jacket
Stocking cap
Gloves
Muffler

Shoes
Sport coat
White shirt
Tie
3/4 coat
Sox
Belt

EMIL ILCHAK

Trousers
Undershirt-l.s.
Unbuttoned neckband shirt
Suspenders
Shoes
Sox
Pocket watch
Wedding band
Vest
Pullover sweater

Mackinaw
Fedora
Gloves

Collar
Tie
Suit
Shoes
Shirt

ARDENSHENSKY

3 piece black tweed suit
Collarless shirt
Suspenders
Shoes
Sox
Hat
Overcoat
Gloves
Muffler
Tie
Collar
Pocket watch
Cufflinks

UKRAINIAN PRIEST

Long black robe
Hat

ADDENDUM

If an intermission is required in TODAY, I AM A FOUNTAIN PEN, the following scenes may be inserted into p. 35 of Dramatists Play Service published edition, at the place on the printed page already indicated by an asterisk (*) for such an act break. The following new Act One Irving/Ardenshensky scene is to be inserted immediately after the blackout ending the existing Irving/Annie/Pete scene. Ardenshensky's new Act Two speech will, of course, immediately follow the intermission. Use of this new material is also suggested if producing groups wish to enlarge the role of Ardenshensky. These additions to my play were recently negotiated by my old friend Sol Frieder, a genius of an actor, to whom these new scenes are forever dedicated ... with my love.

Israel Horovitz, NYC
January, 1996.

Irving walks to park bench, where he discovers Mr. Ardenshensky sitting alone, bundled in an old tweed overcoat.

IRVING. Hi.
ARDENSHENSKY. Hi.
IRVING. Quite a storm.
ARDENSHENSKY. Don't tell *me* about snow! I'm an old man!
IRVING. Aren't you Mr. Ardenshensky?
ARDENSHENSKY. Who wants to know?
IRVING. I'm Irving Yanover.
ARDENSHENSKY. Are you related to the dry goods Yanover?
IRVING. He's my father. I've seen you in the shop.
ARDENSHENSKY. Your father sold me a defective sheet.
IRVING. I heard.
ARDENSHENSKY. How did you hear?
IRVING. My bedroom's right over the shop. You were screaming.
ARDENSHENSKY. I never scream. I project. I'm an actor.
IRVING. Where do you act?
ARDENSHENSKY. In Poland.
IRVING. Recently?
ARDENSHENSKY. If I acted in Poland, recently, I'd be dead. And if I were dead, you'd be talking to the Ghost of Allen's Father.
IRVING. Who's Allen?
ARDENSHENSKY. My son.
IRVING. Oh, right. I get it. I'm very interested in things like acting. I'm going to be a concert pianist. Like Horowitz. Do you know Horowitz.
ARDENSHENSKY. The man or the matzoh?
IRVING. The man. He's the greatest pianist on the planet Earth.
ARDENSHENSKY. Better than Arnold Paterofsky?
IRVING. Who's Arnold Paterofsky?
ARDENSHENSKY. My nephew in Winnipeg. *(Ardenshensky sees Irving's mittens aren't on his hands.)* My dear young Mr. Yanover, you'd better put something warm on your hands, unless you're planning to play the piano with your toes. Here ... take my

gloves.
IRVING. I have mittens!
ARDENSHENSKY. Where? Did you lose them?
IRVING. Oh, no, they're right here! *(Shows Ardenshensky his mittens hanging from his mitten-clips.)* It's not possible for me to lose my mittens, unless, of course, I lose my whole coat, which *has* happened, but, not a lot.
ARDENSHENSKY. And a good thing, too. *(Ardenshensky studies Irving's mitten-clips as Irving puts his mittens on his hands.)* Isn't that clever? I should have things like that for my gloves. I mostly lose right hands. Last year, alone, I lost three right hands! I have a cigar box full of left hands. It makes me sick to look in the box!... What are they called, those things?
IRVING. These? Mitten-clips.
ARDENSHENSKY. Mitten-clips? You see that? Jews are the best inventors in the world!
IRVING. I'm sure that's true, but, how do you know for certain that a Jew invented mitten-clips?
ARDENSHENSKY. Just say the word: "Mitten-clips."
IRVING. It does *sound* Jewish.
ARDENSHENSKY. Would a Protestant invent anything called *Mitten-clips?*
IRVING. I see what you mean. I've always assumed that mitten-clips were an English invention, because the words "Mitten" and "Clips" are both English.
ARDENSHENSKY. You think "Mitten" and "Clips" are *English?* Are you a *meshuggena?* I suppose you think "Box-kite" is English!?
IRVING. "Box-kite"? Oh, right ... the kind of kite you fly that looks like a box ... Stanley Rosen has a box-kite that he flies in the park with his mother. Rosen's a jerk. *(Says "Box-kite" aloud, slowly and thoughtfully.)* "Boxxx-kiiiite." *(Smiles.)* I see what you mean, Mr. Ardenshensky. I never really thought about whether or not a box-kite was a *Jewish* invention, before now. Are there many other Jewish words in the English language, Mr. Ardenshensky?
ARDENSHENSKY. You must be joshing! The English language is *full* of Jewish words!

IRVING.   Like what?
ARDENSHENSKY.   There are a million of them!... uhhh, *Bedraggled*.... *Conniption*.... *Fear-laden*. (That's one of my favorites: fear-laden.) Also, the thing you scoop soup with ...
IRVING.   A ladle!
ARDENSHENSKY.   Exactly! You think an Irish Catholic came up with a *ladle!?* ... And, while we're thinking about soup, how about "Lentil"?
IRVING.   Oh, "Lentil" is *definitely* Jewish! *(Irving giggles.)*
ARDENSHENSKY.   What? Something funny?
IRVING.   My mother always adds "Garnish" to the fruit salad. "Garnish" *has* to be Jewish, right?
ARDENSHENSKY.   "Garnish"? *Voo den?*
IRVING.   Oh, I like this! Name some other Jewish words!
ARDENSHENSKY.   "Foible."
IRVING.   What does "Foible" mean?
ARDENSHENSKY.   Nobody knows.
IRVING.   How about "Dental" and "Mental."
ARDENSHENSKY.   What do you think?
IRVING.   Definitely Jewish! I can't imagine two more Jewish-sounding words ... "Dental" ... "Mental".... Ooooo, how about "Snuggle"?
ARDENSHENSKY.   "Snuggle" is Jewish.
IRVING.   *(Suddenly remembers.)* Oh, God! Have we been talking more than six minutes, Mr. Ardenshensky?
ARDENSHENSKY.   Why? You've got a time-limit on talking?
IRVING.   I do, sort of. I promised Annie and Pete I'd take a walk, so they could snuggle and smooch for six minutes, but, then, I'm supposed to come back and get them, so we can leave and get home by 7 o'clock.
ARDENSHENSKY.   Are they the two smoochers on my bench over there?
IRVING.   That's *your* bench?
ARDENSHENSKY.   My *favorite* bench. I was sitting on it, reading my newspaper, when they drove up. I came over here to watch the ferry-boat coming in from Michigan. When I went back to my bench, they were sitting on it, smooching. My newspaper's tucked in the bench-slats beside them, but, I

didn't feel I should interrupt such personal goings-on.... So, that's why I'm stuck waiting here ... 'til they stop smooching. If you can go make them stop smooching and leave, I can get my paper and go home, before my *kishkas* freeze, altogether!
IRVING.   I'll go get them to stop smooching and leave, right away. *(Starts off; stops.)* It was very nice chatting with you, Mr. Ardenshensky.
ARDENSHENSKY.   Likewise.
IRVING.   Do you think "smooch" is a Jewish word?
ARDENSHENSKY.   What do *you* think?
IRVING.   *Voo den?...* Goodnight, Mr. Ardenshensky.
ARDENSHENSKY.   Tell your father I'll be knocking on his door with my defective sheet.
IRVING.   I'll tell him. *(Irving exits.)*
ARDENSHENSKY.   *(To audience.)* Nice boy. He takes after his mother.... We'll take an intermission here. Fifteen minutes. No smooching! *(The lights fade to black.)*

END OF ACT ONE

ACT TWO

Ardenshensky walks out on stage, calls to the Stage Manager, off.

ARDENSHENSKY. House lights out, please. *(House lights begin to fade out. Ardenshensky calls to Audience.)*
 Settle, please! We're starting the second act!... Unwrap all your Act Two hard candy, now, please. Otherwise, you'll do it during a quiet, dramatic moment, slowly, thinking you're being discreet, but, everybody around you will hear the noise of your candy-wrapper, which sounds like a mouse scratching, and they'll think that the [name of theatre] has got a mouse problem. *(Calls to Stage Manager.)*
 May I have my spotlight, please?... *(Spotlight finds Ardenshensky, who is suddenly bathed in pink light. Smiles to Audience; ironically.)*
 Very nice, this color ... if I were dancing in "Swan Lake"! *(Ardenshensky flashes nasty look toward Stage Manager's booth. Spotlight color changes to green. Disgusted.)*
 You *can't* be serious! I'm not playing Dracula! *(Spotlight-color changes to soft flattering neutral tone. Ardenshensky smiles.)*
 Thank you. *(Ardenshensky now talks to Audience, directly.)*
 So, here we are, again.... It's now 1942, and the hideous war is in full swing. Concentration camps are fixtures on the European landscape, like monuments to the Devil, himself. Jews and Gypsies and homosexuals are being exterminated like vermin. The French are fighting side by side with the Allies, but, on the sly, they are selling Hitler their bubbliest champagne, their smoothest *fois gras,* and many thousand lovely French Jews. In divided Italy, brothers are fighting against brothers, but, soon enough, the black-shirted brothers aligned with Mussolini will overpower all ... and Italy and Germany will stand with Japan, against Jews and Gypsies and homosexuals and the rest of the world. It seems unbelievable, now, doesn't it? Well, *believe it,* my friends, *believe it!* Because, if we don't ... if we allow ourselves to forget these horrors of

real-life, we will be condemned to re-live them, again!...
George Santayana and Jacob Ardenshensky swear this to be
true! (*Smiles.*) Real life.... *Oy vay!* Luckily, tonight, we are not
dealing with real life!... (*Lights fade up in Yanover living room,
behind Ardenshensky. Moses sits in his easy-chair, reading the Sunday Newspaper. Radio is on table next to Moses. Esther is in kitchen,
readying the Sunday meal.*)
... We are in the theatre, watching a very nice play
about a very nice Jewish family, the Yanovers, who live in Sault
Ste. Marie, Ontario, Dominion of Canada, three thousand five
hundred miles away from the hideous War. (*Calls to Moses.*)

We're almost ready, Mr. Yanover. (*Moses smiles at
Ardenshensky. Ardenshensky says his goodbye to the Audience.*)

I think you'll enjoy the second act even more than the
first act. It's more *conclusive.* The first act wanders a bit; the
second act moves dramatically.... It's lean. To use a Jewish
word ... it's *svelt.* (*Remembers.*)

Oh, yes.... You'll be seeing me, again, in the second
act. I washed the defective sheet Yanover pawned off on me
in Dreft, the Jewish detergent, and the sheet fell apart, altogether. This, I cannot live with! (*Ardenshensky nods to Moses.*)

Okay, Mr. Yanover ... hit it! (*Ardenshensky exits, as lights
shift to Moses. Radio Announcer's voice fades in, under scene.*)
RADIO ANNOUNCER.   The Suez Canal is seriously threatened by a surprise Nazi attack. The first meeting of German
and British armies is being fought now on the deserts of North
Africa ...
MOSES.   I don't like what I read in my Sunday paper!
RADIO ANNOUNCER.   ... On these same grounds, the British forces had their first victory, with a three hundred mile
mechanized walk across Italian Libya, capturing and killing one
hundred thousand Italians ...
MOSES.   And I don't like what I'm hearing on my radio,
either!

NOTE: Play now continues as printed.

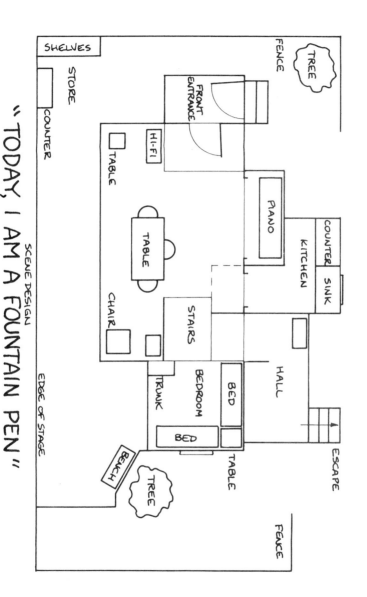

"TODAY, I AM A FOUNTAIN PEN"
SCENE DESIGN
(DESIGNED BY JAMES FENHAGEN FOR THE AMERICAN JEWISH THEATER)

NEW PLAYS

LONELY PLANET
by Steven Dietz

THE AMERICA PLAY
by Suzan-Lori Parks

THE FOURTH WALL
by A.R. Gurney

JULIE JOHNSON
by Wendy Hammond

FOUR DOGS AND A BONE
by John Patrick Shanley

DESDEMONA, A PLAY ABOUT A HANDKERCHIEF
by Paula Vogel

Write for information as to availability
DRAMATISTS PLAY SERVICE, Inc.
440 Park Avenue South   New York, N.Y. 10016